Seeing History:
Public History in
Britain Now

Edited by Hilda Kean, Paul Martin
and Sally J. Morgan

Seeing History: Public History in Britain Now

Francis
Boutle
Publishers

First published by Francis Boutle Publishers
23 Arlington Way
London EC1R 1UY
Tel/Fax: (020) 7278 4497
Email: seeinghistory@francisboutle.demon.co.uk
www.francisboutle.demon.co.uk

Copyright © Contributors, 2000

All rights reserved.
No part of this book may be reproduced, stored
in a retrieval system, or transmitted, in any form
or by any means, electronic, mechanical
photocopying or otherwise without the prior permission
of the publishers.

ISBN 0 9532388 9 X

Printed in Great Britain by Redwood Books

Acknowledgements

The illustration of the painting by Sir Gerald Kelly of Queen Elizabeth, the Queen Mother and the photograph of Daphne Du Maurier by Bassano are reproduced by courtesy of the National Portrait Gallery, London. The illustration of the red squirrel postage stamp is reproduced by kind permission of The Post Office. All rights reserved. The photographs of Swindon Road Cottages, Avebury, are reproduced by kind permission of Heather Peak-Garland. The illustrations 'Respect Earned' and 'Murphy's Law' are taken from *Waitemata Ferry Tales* by Jim Storey and Sally Fodie, published by Ferry Boat Publishers, Auckland, 1995, and are reproduced with the permission of the authors. The photograph 'Women preparing the fish for curing at Grimsby' is from the exhibition Unsung Voices at the National Fishing Heritage Centre, Grimsby, 1999, and is reproduced by permission of the Centre. The photograph of the Bishopsgate Institute in advance of its formal opening, 1894, is reproduced courtesy of the Guildhall Library; the map of the eastern half of the City of London and the bookplate of the Bishopsgate Library by Walter Crane are reproduced by kind permission of the Bishopsgate Institute. In a few cases we have been unable to trace copyright holders; we would be grateful to hear from anyone we have inadvertently failed to credit.

Hilda Kean, Paul Martin, Sally J. Morgan

Contents

- 9   Contributors
- 11 List of illustrations
- 13 Introduction.
  Hilda Kean, Paul Martin and
  Sally J. Morgan
- 19 My father's photographs: the visual as public history.
  Sally J. Morgan
- 37 History, family, history.
  Tim Brennan
- 51 Save 'our' red squirrel: kill the American grey tree rat.
  Hilda Kean
- 65 Avebury and not-so-ancient places: the making of the English heritage landscape.
  Brian Edwards
- 81 Putting gender into seafaring: representing women in public maritime history.
  Jo Stanley
- 105 Language and landscape: the construction of place in an East London borough.
  Bruce Wheeler

127 'But it's not all nostalgia': public history and local identity in Birmingham.
Paul Long

151 Managing boundaries: history and community at the Bishopsgate Institute.
Peter Claus

171 Sound judgements: the compact disc reissue scene as Public History.
Paul Martin

190 Index

Contributors

Tim Brennan studied Fine Art at Hull and the Slade, and Public History at Ruskin College. He works in a variety of artistic forms – performance, writing, sculpture, new technology, sound, photography – as well as working as a curator and teacher. He was Artistic Leader of W139 Gallery in Amsterdam and worked for Camerawork in East London. Formerly Assistant Director of MA Fine Art Curating at Goldsmiths' College, he is currently Artistic Director of Arthouse Multimedia Centre for the Arts in Dublin.

Peter Claus is an associate lecturer and course consultant at the Open University where he took his PhD. He has published and given papers on the political and cultural life of the Victorian City of London in which he has a passionate interest since researching the closure of Spitalfields market while a Ruskin student. He is currently writing a book on public health in the Victorian city and collating the Raphael Samuel archive at the Bishopsgate Institute.

Brian Edwards is currently researching a PhD in History at the University of the West of England. He is a contributor to *Wiltshire Folklife*, *Babbling Brook*, *Wiltshire Archaeological Magazine*, *Regional Historian* and *History Workshop Journal*. Forthcoming publications include a chapter in *Orwell in Context: Essays New and Recent*, edited by Peter Davison, and an article in *Nature First: the Journal of the Natural History Museum*.

Hilda Kean is a tutor in History and course director of the MA in Public History at Ruskin College. Her latest books are *Animal Rights. Social and Political Change in Britain since 1800* (Reaktion Books, 1998) and (edited with Geoff Andrews and Jane Thompson) *Ruskin College. Contesting Knowledge, Dissenting Politics* (Lawrence and Wishart, 1999). She is currently researching family and local history in East London.

Paul Long has lived all his life in Birmingham and is finally contemplating a move away – to Hull. He is visiting lecturer at the University of Central England where he teaches Media Studies. As a research student at the University of Warwick he is currently completing his doctorate on class and culture in post-war Britain.

Paul Martin is visiting lecturer in Material Culture at the Department of Museum Studies, University of Leicester and is a tutor in History at Ruskin College. He is the author of *Popular Collecting and the Everyday Self: the Reinvention of Museums?* (Leicester University Press, 1999). His latest books are *The Trade Union Badge. Material Culture in Action* and, with Susan Pearce, *The Collectors' Voice Vol IV: Contemporary Collecting* (both to be published by Ashgate Press in 2001). He is currently researching the history and cultures of consumption and community in post-war popular music in Britain.

Sally J. Morgan is principal lecturer in Fine Arts and course leader of the MA 'Fine Art in Context' at the University of the West of England, Bristol. She is a practising artist and archaeologist. She studied Fine Art at the Royal Academy, Antwerp and Public History at Ruskin College at post-graduate level, and her work reflects the meeting of these two discourses. Her published work has concentrated on the 'visual' in public history and popular memory.

Jo Stanley is a writer and historian whose writings on women and the sea are widely published. A lecturer at Leeds, Manchester and Bradford Universities, she is currently working on a book on stewardesses on liners at the Institute for Cultural Research, Lancaster University. She holds a Research Fellowship at the University of Warwick Modern Records Centre and is co-ordinator of the international Women and the Sea Network, based at the National Maritime Museum. Art-school trained and interested in inter-disciplinarity, she paints, writes fiction, and makes videos and exhibitions.

Bruce Wheeler is currently a post-graduate student at Birkbeck College where he is researching nineteenth century British social history, in particular the rise of science and its impact on working class cultures and beliefs. He lives and works in Newham in East London.

List of illustrations

Page 25   Mary Jane Morgan

Page 27   Queen Elizabeth, the Queen Mother by Sir Gerald Kelly, 1938

Page 29   Daphne Du Maurier

Page 30   Dai Morgan and a group of officers and sergeants of the 10 South Wales Borderers, circa 1918

Page 53   1977 postage stamp featuring a red squirrel

Page 70   Swindon Road cottages before and during demolition

Page 82   Murphy's Law by Jim Storey and Sally Fodie

Page 85   Respect earned by Jim Storey and Sally Fodie

Page 93   Women preparing the fish for curing at Grimsby

Page 110 Extract of Chapman and André's map of the County of Essex, 1777

Page 150 Bishopsgate Institute before its formal opening in 1894

Page 153   Map of the eastern half of the City of London showing the Bishopsgate Institute and the limit of the lending Department of the Library, 1894

Page 160   Bishopsgate Library bookplate by Walter Crane, circa 1894

Introduction

Hilda Kean, Paul Martin, Sally J. Morgan

In recent years Public History – the engagement with history now – has grown in Britain. Visits to heritage sites, museums and galleries are key leisure activities. Interest in family and local history is growing so fast that archive departments have scant space to accommodate researchers. History programmes on television and radio, including the new satellite channel devoted to the topic, are increasingly popular. Most of this work is taking place outside the traditional sites of research, universities. Indeed, David Cannadine, director of the Institute of Historical Research in London has bemoaned the lack of significant work by professional colleagues. Pioneer feminist and social historian Sheila Rowbotham has despaired at the inward looking nature of academic history and longed for a return to engagement between the academy and the real world. This collection is an attempt to bridge that gap between the academy and popular history.

Public History acts as an umbrella, under which the historical mind can be brought to bear on areas of research and thought which are too often seen as mutually exclusive. It draws upon the magazine racks of W.H.Smith for source material as much as it draws on academic texts. It looks as much to images and textual conceptions on commercial packaging and television advertising as it does to the art gallery and museum. It seeks oral opinion conveyed through the domestic images recorded by camcorder, constructed images and visual texts on television, and the holistic nature of the idea of knowledge expressed by the Internet. Public History relies on a collective and collaborative effort of people often working in different fields. This very process, of itself, helps to avoid academic navel gazing. In examining the 'historical self' in the context of our perception of time and sense of place, for instance, the necessity for the enlargement of our terms of reference becomes apparent. In collaborative efforts such as the creation of this book, the shaping and interpretation as well as the experience of events provides a broad and democratic way of seeing, all too often sacrificed on the altar of personal kudos in conventional academic history.

What is noteworthy about recent years is the way in which social and cultural certainties and boundaries have dissolved. Part of what Public History is about, in this sense, is to trace the ways in which such clearly defined borders have been reconfigured or abandoned altogether while challenging the validity of the absolutes that they were held to represent.

In the 1970s the History Workshop movement under the aegis of Raphael Samuel, tutor in history at Ruskin College, Oxford, led the field in new history, 'history from below', based on democratic scholarship, which engaged with the familiar and intervened in public debates about the direction of history in schools and national life. In recent years this work has been continued in different ways, particularly through courses encouraging links between the academy and popular history and inviting personal engagement with the day-to-day: personal collections, family albums, place and landscape, heritage and museums, history in film and television. On a microcosmic scale, the interests around everyday encounters and perceptions of personally experienced history, the hegemony of the tried and tested (the old) over the perceived vacuousness of the new, which in any case seems constantly to reference itself to the past, are the sites of the public historians' 'coalface'.

English Heritage's recent listing of a 1950s Durham miner's pigeon loft, and its mounting of a 'blue plaque' on the London home of Jimi Hendrix, together with the National Trust's listing of Paul McCartney's childhood terraced council house, are proof of the ways in which the popular is informing the conventionally elite. To disseminate this approach to history more widely a Public History discussion group was established in 1998, meeting regularly in Oxford to discuss a broad range of current historical topics. This publication is a result of these seminars and discussions.

What unites the different contributors of *Seeing History* is our commitment to the practice of history now, be it analysis of local landscapes and buildings, the marketing of heritage, the intricacies of the making of public history, or the blurring of boundaries between the academy and the world. Unsurprisingly, visual images form a significant part of this book and in a sense provide a unity of process. For what is seen and what is experienced in our everyday lives is as likely to be as significant in our understanding and creation of history as the reading of books or archives.

The various contributors are consciously blurring the edges between different narrow discourses of history and revisiting ideas either relegated to academic practice or dismissed as the concern of enthusiastic amateurs. Thus Sally Morgan and Tim Brennan in their respective chapters explore in rather different ways their own family histories. Morgan's starting point is a selection of photographs compiled for her by her father shortly before his death; for Brennan it is a diary written during the course of 1914 and passed down through his mother's family. The text of the photographs and the very physical existence of the diary are put to use to make links with and challenge the more usual practice of rummaging in local archives to discover family origins and to construct family histories. We are also concerned with the way in which ideas of heritage have been developed and used in different ways. So Hilda Kean considers the way in which the red squirrel has been appropriated as a symbol of Englishness, while Brian Edwards looks critically at the construction of the world heritage site of Avebury in Wiltshire. As Edwards argues, the Avebury ring as we see it now owes more to the enthusiasm of a 1930s marmalade manufacturer than to masons of many thousands of years ago.

Other contributors write about places they know well, not just from delving in the archives but from lived experience. The starting point for several of them is what they see around them in their daily lives and a desire to explore such surroundings critically. History becomes then not part of a past which has gone but part of a living present constantly being re-created, contested and challenged. Links are made between the personal and the public, expanding the boundaries of historical knowledge and individual experience. In his chapter, Paul Long, who identifies himself as a 'Brummy', discusses the way in which 'Birmingham' has constructed a particular identity for itself. His concern is with who is included and excluded from such a project and raises questions about the boundaries of history, culture, nation and locality. In different vein Bruce Wheeler considers the way in which Newham in East London has been defined and redefined as a particular place through shifts and changes in language. Jo Stanley draws on her position, as she defines it, as the female child of Liverpool seafarers to consider the absence of women and gender relations from maritime history particularly that publicly displayed in galleries. For Stanley this absence matters, 'because I feel hurt, excluded, angry and confused when confronted by omission of a history that I know exists. I assume that a public site of knowledge should show what I know from personal experience to be the case'.

While all the contributors develop ideas of Public History which challenge preconceived notions of the relationship between the academic and the amateur, Paul Martin and Peter Claus explore explicitly the notion of where and how historical knowledge is created. Claus analyses the role of the Bishopsgate Institute created in London in the 1890s as both a welfare and educational initiative. Unlike nearly all its contemporaries the Institute still exists today. Physically it sits on the borders of the City of London and metaphorically on the margins between the unofficial knowledge of its bizarre archive and the official siting of the Centre for Metropolitan History founded by the social historian Raphael Samuel shortly before his death in 1996. In contrast, it is not in a library that Paul Martin situates his chapter but within music magazines like *Mojo* and *Record Collector*, which he describes as the public history journals of the high street magazine racks. With the reissuing of vintage music on compact disc and the proliferation of television programmes such as 'Rock Family Trees' Martin sees an informal musical open university having been created. As he suggests, 'people become intellectually primed for history, even without recognising it'.

As we said, in certain respects an impetus for our work in Public History had been the History Workshop initiative of the 1970s. Although it is unlikely that any of the chapters included here would have been so conceived some thirty years ago, nevertheless many of the concerns of that earlier period are still our concerns. These include an allegiance to those whose lives are still excluded from historical practice and a commitment to a praxis which places emphasis on what is being said rather than to the status of who is saying it. We hope that this collection will illustrate in practical ways the continuing importance of acknowledging that images of the past need to be recognised by the present as our own concerns if they are not to disappear irretrievably.

My father's photographs: the visual as Public History

Sally J. Morgan

Families build a sense of themselves, and of their place in the world, through the construction of narratives and the passing on of stories attached to pictures, artefacts and rituals.[1] Nations do likewise through the writing of history. The domestic photographic collection is a place where each generation marks the role of both big public events, war or economic depression, and small private ones, marriages or births, in the shaping of a family's identity. This kind of record represents the place where autobiography meets 'History'; where small stories interweave with bigger ones, subjectivity and objectivity jostle for ascendancy, and, 'meaning' becomes narrative.[2]

Not long before he was diagnosed as having terminal cancer, my father, Trevor Morgan, assembled a small collection of photographs and had them reproduced for his children. I intend to show that mnemonic artefacts, such as my father's set of photographs, may be read in conjunction with other evidence to give us an understanding of personal, family, community and public history. My argument is that, in common with many family albums, my father's photographs, are a deliberate, historical 'text' in which meaning has been placed. I am not, I believe, dealing with an introspective, sub-specialism of history. These 'informal' histories have significance beyond the apparently private world of 'Family History'. Broad social meaning may be found in these 'vernacular' cultural productions and they are important in helping us to find the 'connections between big changes and the distinctive experiences of particular social milieux'.[3]

A visual history
In 1990 Trevor had been having headaches for some time. These were so bad that he would go and stand in the garden during the night in the hope that the chilly air would reduce the pain. At some point during that year he went through the drawer of photographs that he kept in the front room, and made a small selection. He then asked his youngest daughter's boyfriend, a photographer, to make copies for his children. Although I don't remember how I received the package, I do remember holding a large, crease-free brown envelope and being surprised that he'd gone to such trouble. It was a sunny day, South Devon light pouring through my window onto photographs of faces familiar only in their resemblance to ourselves: my father's mouth on his father's face; my brother's smile coming, disconcertingly, from a man he never knew.

Today I sit with the photographs around me as I write. Occasionally I hold one in my hands, allowing it to open doors in my memory and my imagination. Once these images were kept loose in a drawer in my grandmother's sideboard. In my memory the drawer opens with a smell of stale perfume, as affecting to me as the smell of raisins was to French philosopher Gaston Bachelard when he remembered a cupboard in his childhood home.[4] In this sourly scented remembered drawer, photographs and random objects rattle around amongst half-burned birthday candles and broken beads. Every object has a story; every photograph becomes a history. I remember times when I looked at this picture before, I remember the different people who looked at it with me. The light begins to fade and I turn on the table lamp, I put on my new reading glasses, I stare at the picture. I remember. I make and extract stories. When Trevor compiled this collection he was in his late sixties, an active, stocky Welshman with thick brown hair and a propensity for running up and down ladders. He looked like a healthy person who might possibly live forever. Nevertheless, I was only slightly surprised by the sudden bequest of these photographs. It passed through my mind that he was making preparations for a time when he would no longer be there and that he was beginning the construction of his own history.

In *Theatres of Memory*, the historian Raphael Samuel speaks of 'the valedictory note of leave taking which turns the photographic album into a kind of elegy for the dead', and of 'the role of photography as a commemorative art – the quality which brings it closest to the spirit of the historian's project'.[5] My father seemed to be very well aware of these qualities in the material that he was handing on to us. At the time I was amused by it all, thinking that it was typical of him to do something like *that* before it was necessary, but to leave the stairs unrepaired until they fell down. He seemed preoccupied with the past and the future, but oblivious to the present. As it turned out, in less than two years he was dead. Diagnosed on 26 November 1991 with two brain-tumours, he died on 26 May 1992 in the Taylor Memorial Home, Birmingham. The uncreased package full of the few images that he had chosen to indicate the fact of his existence became painfully significant. Now my grief and memory was overlaid on his, and a new layer of meaning was added to his photographic 'text'.

Personal and public meaning
Patricia Holland, in her 1997 essay, 'How Sweet it is to Scan', talks about two different positions from which a viewer might attempt to understand a photograph. One may be compared to the theory of French writer and critic Roland Barthes of private meaning in relation to photography, which he called the 'punctum',[6] the other to his 'studium',[7] the public, or culturally constructed meaning in a photograph. Holland talks about 'users' and 'readers'. According to her argument a user of a photograph would be someone, like my father, who uses the image as a personal mnemonic device. She tells us that:

Users of personal pictures have access to the world in which they make sense; readers must translate those private meanings into a more public realm.[8]

My position was possibly somewhere between these two, a user required by circumstance to become a reader. My task as a reader was also complex. I felt I needed to read the photographs on at least two levels. The first in terms of my father's intention and secondly in terms of the more general cultural meanings constructed through the image. An added complication was, of course, my own 'punctum', the particular associations of the photograph that provided meaning for me alone.

However, while Barthes seems to argue, in *Camera Lucida*, that the personal meaning that exists in and around all photography undermines its shareable, culturally constructed meaning, and his later critics like Burgin[9] and Mitchell,[10] seem to find an intellectually crippling paradox in this assertion, I am not convinced by this argument. It doesn't seem problematic to me that both these things exist simultaneously in the photographic 'text'. Dissonance is not, perforce, paradox. The idea of the 'punctum' could as easily be applied to the poem, the novel, or any other mimetic form, describing perceptual experience. I would contend that all 'imaging', all description, like my earlier invocation of South Devon light, holds within it the possibility of the personal 'wound' of private connotation. This does not deny or disprove intended meaning, it simply acknowledges the additional accretions of significance that adhere to all cultural products, be they written texts, images or artefacts. Some are easier to uncover than others are, but more than one set of meanings exists in and around the image at one and the same time. When I first began looking at my father's photographs I felt as though he had given me the elements of his story, but not its matrix. I suspected that we had been set some task. But now, from this distance, I can see that, in fact, the matrix was there all along; that the images were meant to be read singly, sequentially, and as a whole. The line through the images was time, and the narrative was both autobiographical and historical, both carefully public and intensely personal.

Story containers

After his diagnosis with a terminal brain tumour, when he had been brought home and lay in what had been my teenage bedroom, my father asked to speak to me. It was to be the last coherent conversation that we had, and amid all the talk, all the stripping away, and the piling on, of pretence and bravado, he exposed what seemed to be his greatest fear – that he would be forgotten, that there would be no stories about him and his life left in the world, that he would simply disappear. I promised that I wouldn't forget, and implicit in that pledge was the assurance that I would also *tell*; that I would be the conduit for his text, that his memory would go beyond me. This may be what turned me into an historian; the weight of my father's fear of his own transience, his urge towards some kind of immortality, his need to figure in a story. He didn't have the money to build monuments to himself, or the social standing to have institutions named after him. His 'mnemonic devices',[11] his 'story-containers', were the possessions he handed on to me and to my sisters and brothers; visual texts in the form of photographs.

The photographs that Trevor chose were as follows:
1. a picture of his father and two uncles as young men;
2. a group of soldiers of the South Wales Borderers Regiment which included my grandfather in the front row [page 30];
3. my grandmother, in what appears to be her thirties [page 25];
4. himself, in RAF uniform aged about eighteen, inscribed 'To Mam and Dad, with all my love, Trev.';
5. my parents' wedding photograph;
6. me, his eldest child, aged four or five;
7. a group-portrait of four of his five children;
8. a picture of my brother, David, my junior by eight years, and myself. We are sitting on my nanna's backsteps in Abertillery, South Wales. He is aged about two and I am about to give him a chocolate from a box of Cadbury's Roses.

Apart from time, what are the threads that run through this selection? What seemed so significant about these images that Trevor chose them above all others to be handed on to his children? Only one of the photographs is a snapshot, the last one. The rest are posed and taken by professional photographers, even the picture of me aged four or five, sitting on the chair in the living room, was taken by a local photographer who came to our house to capture my sister Jane and myself for posterity. I remember it clearly, it was an occasion, although then (and now) I failed to understand what happened to make my parents want to formally record that moment. Of all the hundreds of informal, amateur shots that my father and other relatives had documented our lives with, only one has achieved the special status of being ritually handed on, the picture of me with my brother. As I examine the pictures I begin to think that this photo is an aside, a personal message to me. The others, the formally posed portraits, are the history that my father has constructed and which he wants me to show to the world.

Exploring the 'studium'
The fact that the photographs of my grandparents and great-

uncles were taken by studio photographers doesn't seem at all surprising to me. I assume that they didn't have cameras until later in life, because I've never seen any 'home-made' photographs of them before their middle-age. I have no recollection of seeing a photograph of my father as a child in the 1920s. Until the ubiquitous Box Brownie camera became cheap enough for the average working class family, photography still lay largely in the hands of the specialist. Patricia Holland tells us that by the 1920s it was affordable by 'all but the poorest'[12] families. My father's family must have qualified as the poorest, because they clearly didn't possess one, although I suspect that factors other than poverty must have played some part in this absence of casual images. Whatever the reason, the photograph, in the youth of my grandparents, was most certainly an event. It was not an instantaneous record of a piece of unselfconscious, accidentally observed spontaneity. It was posed, an effort had to be made to remain still if the image was not to be a blur.

Fox Talbot, the pioneer Victorian photographer, wrote about the construction of 'delightful pictures' through artifice, that is, through 'arrangement', and 'immobility'.[13] Every muscle in the subject's body was self-consciously controlled in order to construct an image. Nothing was innocently recorded in passing because of the necessity for the subject to remain motionless for a given period of time. Indeed, early photographers often used unseen metal scaffolds and clamps to hold people in place from behind while the picture was being taken. In this stillness an image is consciously constructed between the photographer and the photographed. I think that it may also be argued that even when sustained immobility was no longer necessary, the habit of studied, self-conscious, self-composition remained, as did the complicity with the photographer. The subject has chosen, usually, 'to look their best' and the photographer has contracted, implicitly, to 'show them at their best'. The decision about what constitutes 'best' is of course complex and influenced by a mixture of social expectation and personal fantasy.[14]

As Roland Barthes observes: 'I constitute myself in the process of "posing"... I lend myself to the social game, I pose, I know I am posing, I want you to know that I am posing.'[15] When my grandmother posed, half-turned towards the camera, her hair in a Marcel wave, a string of costume pearls

Mary Jane Morgan [photographer unknown]

around her neck, her glasses nowhere to be seen, and her shoulders partially revealed through the lacy sleeves of her dress, she and the photographer had colluded in the production of a readable, public, 'studium' in which she was constructed, for the moment, within the parameters of a mutually agreed template. That moment was one that would live beyond her death and would therefore be one of the few moments that would define her historically. The truth about this image is that it *is* an image of my grandmother, Mary Jane Morgan, a constructed image in which many of the social facts about her appear to be fudged or obscured. If one were Holland's reader rather than a user,[16] one might find it very difficult to deduce specifics from this image. It is a picture of a woman, and by the appearance of her dress and hairstyle we might be able to approximate the decade in which the photograph was taken.

As a user of this image, however, as someone with access to supplementary information, I am able to make other readings. I know that she has taken her glasses off. I know that the pearls are fake, I know that the brooch contains no precious metals or stones. I know that, like Carolyn Steedman's mother in *Landscape for a Good Woman*,[17] she is a working-class woman with aspirations. I know that this photograph represents what she would like to be in terms of social status, rather than what she is. I think that that in itself tells me something about her and something about the lives of working-class women at that time. This is a construct of her desire, or an optical manifestation of it. She is not depicted, she conceives herself according to her aspirations. In this sense the photograph becomes an idea rather than a mimetic device through which we observe an innocent reality. This is a space where a woman can say, 'this is what I ought to be,' as a substitute for, 'this is what I fear I am'. The image is not constructed by the hired photographer, but with and through him. He becomes in a sense an 'interlocutor'.[18]

Thus it may be argued the images my father has chosen to represent his history are mostly those in which meaning had been deliberately constructed by the sitters in collaboration with a professional photographer who had access to the structural rules of a visual code. In the construction of these images very little has been allowed to accident. What is presented is a history of aspiration; a history of what we 'should have been'. This is a view of the working class from within, images that are different from those of the working class from without.[19] Rather than 'the dignity of labour', an external construction, an interpretation of someone else's lived experience, it reveals the dignity of dreams, a manifestation of desire. As Jo Spence maintained: 'All photographs are message carriers, either between members of the same class who share common codes, or between differing classes and cultures ... most of these messages are class biased.'[20] If I compare this studio photograph of my grandmother with that of women of other

Seeing History: Public History in Britain Now 27

Elizabeth, the Queen Mother by Sir Gerald Kelly, 1938

classes from the inter-war years, I begin to see more clearly the subtleties of construction. I also begin to see that what I had previously felt to be invisible in the image becomes discernible. The photograph is coded, there is a language there to be read, but like all languages it must be learnt.

Sir Gerald Kelly's 1938 portrait of Queen Elizabeth the Queen Mother [above] shows us a woman as far removed socially from my grandmother as it may be possible to be.[21] Elizabeth Bowes-Lyon was born into a Scottish aristocratic family and married royalty. She belongs to the class who employed the likes of my family to work in their kitchens. Indeed, my grandmother's younger sister, Doll, spent her whole working life preparing food for the upper classes, finishing her career as cook to the Duke of Bedford. Thousands of women like her and my grandmother, what Gwyn A. Williams called Wales' 'maiden tribute',[22] left Welsh working class homes and worked and lived as servants in the houses of the English gentry and aristocracy. This brought them into very close contact with what may be described as their 'aspirational objects'. They observed some of the signs and insignia associated with wealth and status, and, I would argue, they developed out of them a subset of signs and insignia that mimicked the originals. But these imitations are flawed because the code that is being simulated has not been fully understood and so they either become parody or they omit vital elements.

The conventions of the portrait
In the royal portrait and the photograph of my grandmother we can see the similarities in the women's appearance. Each wears an off the shoulder dress, a brooch at the bosom, an identical hairstyle, and a string of jewels around the neck. However, even though the camera doesn't know that everything that Mary Jane Morgan wears is an imitation, there are ways of discerning the essential difference – the difference of class. Only one of the women, Mary Jane, looks directly at the camera, and only one smiles, also Mary Jane. If we take another portrait [opposite] from about the same time, this time of an upper middle-class woman, we see further subtleties in this code. This woman, Daphne Du Maurier, is not only upper-middle class, she is also famous. She doesn't look at the camera and doesn't smile. She wears no jewellery and her clothes are simple and unadorned. She eschews the flashy vulgarity of adornment associated with the public display of aristocratic or royal power as well as the cheap imitation of these signs of status.

Why is it that when I look at all these photographs that I feel that the images themselves reveal the women's class? The devil, as they say, is in the detail. This is not the kind of detail that Barthes, as discussed earlier, calls the 'punctum', the detail that he contends is outside the culturally constructed

Dame Daphne Du Maurier by Bassano, 24 July 1930

meaning in the image, and which undermines it by producing personal, emotional and thereby idiosyncratic readings. The details I speak about here are very much part of the 'studium'. Each of these images contains details that are deliberate emblems of class, both in their presence and in their absence. My grandmother's class is signified by presence: the presence of paste jewellery, the presence of a smile, the presence of eye contact with the lens and, by implication, the viewer beyond the lens; a kind of direct contact that asks for approval.

Dai Morgan [extreme left, first row] and a group of officers and sergeants of 10 South Wales Borderers circa 1918

However, absence; of jewellery, of a smile, of eye contact, is what signifies Daphne Du Maurier's class. What is asked for here is not approval, but deference. She looks up and away, past us to something more important. This is not the case with Mary Jane. We see her straight on, her gaze meets ours, she seems to see us. She smiles and reveals her teeth, which John Berger, in *Ways of Seeing*, observes that 'the rich in pictures never do'.[23] He notes that the ambassadors in Holbein's well-known painting are:

Both aloof and wary. They expect no reciprocity. They wish the image of their presence to impress others with their...distance.[24]

The images we have seen of upper class women continue this convention. A similar phenomenon can be seen in the regimental photograph of the South Wales Borderers in which my grandfather, Dai Morgan, in his sergeant's stripes, a ribbon of decoration clearly visible above his breast pocket, looks straight into the camera with a smile hovering at the edges of his mouth. All the soldiers in the picture, almost to a man, do likewise. However, one man stands out like a sore thumb, there is something odd about him. In the centre of the photograph sits the man I take to be the Commanding Officer. What has drawn my attention is not that he is obviously older than the rest of the men, nor that he has one leather strap running diagonally across his chest while the others each have two extending like braces from shoulder to waist. What draws my attention to him is the fact that his stance is different, and oddly, his head seems bigger. I realise that he alone of the gathering is leaning forward, slightly turned, and looking to his left. His stance, I begin to understand, denotes his status. Like Daphne Du Maurier and like the Queen Mother, he turns his face away and gazes to our right. I take him to be the company Colonel. I take him to be an officer and a gentleman, and I come to this conclusion even before I discern his age and the trappings of rank. I come to this conclusion because he is centrally placed, leans forward, looks away to his left and does not smile. Richard Leppert has noted that the smile, in European painting, served as a sign of: 'Social irresponsibility (which) set off the child from the adult and the lower social order from its, responsible, hierarchically superior other.' It was considered to be something that: 'tells us the wrong thing about important people, in that it undermined a sense of social power'.[25] The officer at the centre of the photograph, in his refusal to smile and his gaze to the left, does not acknowledge my presence; I am not important enough; he does not seek my approval.

This turning away, this looking into the distance as a pictorial indication of social power can be seen in English pictures of kings and of warriors since as far back as the anonymous 1472 portrait of Edward IV in the Queen's Collection. It is a motif that occurs over and over again. It is particularly noticeable in portraits of the Victorian period. In London's National Portrait Gallery the rooms holding the nineteenth century collection are full of portraits of important people who neither smile at you, nor meet your gaze. Those who do look at you do so severely; those who smile do not look at you. This convention, in which the powerful underline their superiority by not addressing the presence of the audience, became an orthodoxy which was transferred from painting to photography in the late nineteenth century, and reached its height in the first half of the twentieth century.

In the nineteenth century collection of the National Portrait Gallery I came across very few portraits where the central figure smiled directly at the viewer. Where the subject does smile directly at the audience this is not accidental and has particular meaning. Lady Colin Campbell, famed for her sexual exploits, seduces the onlooker, whilst Lord Baden-Powell, founder of the Boy Scout movement, sits and smiles directly at someone at his eye level, intimating that he is perhaps welcoming a reticent child into his company. These two portraits, however, are noteworthy because of their deviation from the norm. In most portraits famous men and women ignore us, or sternly interrogate us with their gaze. In the early twentieth century collection we come across a few more smiling portraits, where parted lips show teeth and/or the gaze is direct. But, interestingly, these sitters are all of people who come from working-class or lower middle-class backgrounds, and were associated with the vulgar sphere of entertainment. They include the Lancashire mezzo-soprano Kathleen Ferrier, the Yorkshire actor and director Charles Laughton, and Alfred Hitchcock the film director. It isn't until the 1960s that we begin to see a breakdown of this code amongst the powerful and, gradually, even royalty begin to smile toothily at the viewer in formal portraits as well as in informal 'snaps'. However, this was not yet the case when my grandparents were formally photographed in the first half of the twentieth century. When, sometime during the inter-war years, my grandmother looked straight at the camera and smiled with her teeth and her Woolworth's pearls bared, she unconsciously followed a visual code that revealed the very thing that I suspect that she was trying to hide; her class.

Messages from a dead father
In this first exploration of the meaning of my father's photographs I have looked mainly at the cultural constructions that helped to convey power, class and aspiration in portrait photography in the inter-war years in Britain. For instance, I have discovered something general and periodised, something *public* in a personal photograph of an ordinary woman, my grandmother. Her very ordinariness reveals something about a moment in history and about a society still confident, at that time, in its social hierarchy. Even though her mock pearls and fancy frock tells us something about her aspirations, the models that inspired those aspirations were members of the moneyed upper classes, who at that time retained a visual code of representation in their portraiture that was designed to under-

line their social superiority.

However, this is only one of the narratives that arise from this set of photographs. Under, or over, the cool and rational, public, narrative in this visual history there run emotional messages from my dead father. This is the 'punctum' again, existing as a secret message amongst all the other, culturally constructed messages and stories that the photograph either contains, or points to. For Barthes the image of his dead mother was the one that produced the idea of the 'punctum', and it is the picture of my dead father, and pictures that symbolise his relationship to myself, that produce the same effect on me. The 'studium' is there in these photographs, but it struggles incessantly with the surges of meaning that come to me through the emotion that, to concur with Linda Orr,[26] makes me want to write at all. In the end though, I see both of them; both 'studium' and 'punctum', and each set of stories has a particular value in the larger scheme of things. My father's photographs are 'a space made up of endless proliferating meanings', and this meaning, as Anton Ehrenzweig put it when talking about the 'hidden order of Art', is 'polyphonic; it evolves not in a single strand of thought, but in several superimposed strands at once'.[27] The emotional strand is as important an element as any other, as much as any thing else, it is a starting point for all other explorations. Trevor began to make this work, I believe, from an emotional standpoint: emotions that stemmed from his knowledge of his mortality.

I try to imagine what was he thinking when he sat in our cold front room, a pain in his head that never went away until he died, an array of photographs scattered on the floor before him. What was he deciding as he was picking them up and putting them back down again, shuffling a narrative like a pack of cards? If, as I believe, he was writing history, and generating a process of history, then what was it that he had in mind to have told? Not long before he died he held my hand emphatically, looked me in the eye, and said, as urgently as a dying man could, 'Promise you won't forget.'

I am haunted by the intensity of that plea which seemed to ask me to incorporate his memories into my own. The raw place where 'history' begins is in the fear of oblivion. Out of that fear we begin to look for immortality and for meaning in narrative. We make sense of ourselves and our existence through the stories we leave. As Hayden White observed, life does not behave like a narrative, but we make meaning through narrative and therefore have to construct the events of our lives into a coherent story through which we achieve our own explanation of events, our own 'meaning'.[28] When my father gave me his photographs he was giving me his own narrative of his own life.

The photographs seem like icons; graven images that are confused with the things that they depict; seeming to become or contain them rather than simply being a description of the configuration of light on flesh at a given moment in time. They seem to be them, but they are not; they are mnemonic artefacts. They evoke emotional memory as well as cultural constructions that give meaning to memory. In choosing a set of photographs that includes one of himself he sets himself into the world of ancestors, he becomes an icon, he ensures his own place in a history that he has given form to. Perhaps, however, amongst the polyphony of simultaneous strands that are inherent in the text that he had constructed, it is possible to detect one that is more *instruction* than message, the conferring on his children of the duty to tell stories of his existence beyond his existence. To tell stories using the mnemonic devices that he had bequeathed to them, to explain and to give meaning: to enter into the process of history.

Old Man: (to the Orator) One last time... I believe in you, ...I'm counting on you... to say everything...to bequeath the message.[29]

Notes

My thanks to the South Wales Borderers and Monmouthshire Regimental Museum, Brecon, the National Portrait Gallery, London and to the Ruskin Public History Group.

1. Daniel Bertaux and Paul Thompson (eds), *International Yearbook of Oral History and Life Stories Vol. II., Between Generations*, Oxford University Press, Oxford, 1993, p. 1.
2. See Hayden White's discussion on history and narrative in his influential and controversial book, *Metahistory: The Historical Imagination in Nineteenth Century Europe*, John Hopkins University Press, Baltimore, 1973.
3. Brian Elliott, 'Biography, Family History and the Analysis of Social Change' in Stephen Kendrick, Pat Straw & David McCrone [eds], *Interpreting the Past, Understanding the Present*, Macmillan, London, 1990, p. 63.
4. Gaston Bachelard, *The Poetics of Space*, Beacon Press, London, 1994, pp. 13–14.
5. Raphael Samuel, *Theatres of Memory*, Verso, London, 1994, p. 375.
6. Roland Barthes, *Camera Lucida*, Vintage, London, 1993, p. 27.
7. Ibid. p. 26.

8 Patricia Holland, 'Sweet it is to Scan...Personal Photographs and Popular Photography', in Liz Wells (ed), *Photography: A Critical Introduction*, Routledge, London, 1997, p. 107.
9 Victor Burgin, *The End of Art Theory: Criticism and Postmodernity*, Macmillan, London, 1986, pp. 90–91.
10 W.J.T. Mitchell, *Picture Theory*, University of Chicago Press, Chicago, 1994.
11 M. Christine Boyer, *The City of Collective Memory*, MIT Press. Cambridge, Mass., 1996, p. 343.
12 Holland, 'Sweet', in Wells, *Photography,* p. 128.
13 Ibid. p. 118.
14 Samuel, *Theatres*, pp. 336–367.
15 Barthes, *Camera*, p. 10.
16 Holland, 'Sweet', in Wells, *Photography*, p. 107.
17 Carolyn Steedman, *Landscape for a Good Woman*, Virago, London, 1986, pp. 6–7.
18 I owe my use of this concept to conversations with my colleague Nicholas Lowe, Senior Lecturer in Fine Arts, U.W.E, Bristol.
19 See Samuel, *Theatres*, p. 324.
20 Jo Spence, *Cultural Sniping*, Routledge, London, 1995, p. 39.
21 My thanks to the Ruskin Public History Group (and to Susie Mayhew in particular) for their contribution to the development of my discussion here.
22 Gwyn A. Williams, *When was Wales?*, Penguin, London ,1985, p. 252.
23 John Berger, *Ways of Seeing*, Penguin, London, 1972, p. 104.
24 Ibid. p. 97.
25 Richard Leppert, *Art and the Committed Eye: The Cultural Functions of Imagery*, Westview Press, Boulder, Colorado, 1996, p. 83.
26 Linda Orr, in her essay 'Intimate Images: Subjectivity and History – Stael, Michelet and Toqueville', asserts that 'to miss the emotional intensity of the historical operation is to miss a major part of its meaning'. In Frank Ankersmit and Hans Kellner (eds), *A New Philosophy of History*, Reaktion, London, 1995, p. 90.
27 Anton Ehrenzweig, *The Hidden Order of Art*, Paladin, London, 1970, p. 14.
28 White, 'The Value of Narrativity in the Representation of Reality,' in Appleby et al, *Knowledge*, p. 404.
29 Eugene Ionesco [trans. Martin Crimp], *The Chairs*, Faber & Faber, London, 1997, p. 55.

History, family, history

Tim Brennan

I grew up being *told* stories about my family history, and in such a way that I found I couldn't engage with the information. The more I heard the less I could piece together, so that the whole process became blocked to the point where I held family history and the passing on of stories in contempt. My assumption that the exploration of family history or genealogy was somehow restricted in its empirical value hardened as I became increasingly involved in contemporary art. So, in the late nineties the unconventional 'guided walks' I led through Britain's cities drew on material seemingly far removed from my family background. When I came upon my great-grandfather William Arthur Jewson's diary of 1914 I initially considered it as just another tool with which to construct and compare topographies of London then and London now. I had decided to disregard his role as a semi-professional London musician; his inner world as the son of a successful family of Court Musicians; his common law relationship with the daughter of an artisan and waitress, Lydia; the psychologically precarious world of his son and my grandfather, Gerald Arthur Jewson.[1]

William Arthur Jewson's diary is a pocket book measuring approximately 12 x 8 cms and has a green marbled softback cover of thin card. On either side are two additional flaps so that it might be slipped into a larger casing, perhaps a wallet or binder. The pages are edged with gold leaf and a purple silk ribbon or bookmark is stitched into the spine. All of William Arthur's inscriptions are made in indelible pencil. They form a precise set of notes which plot his daily journeys across the metropolis, from Bedford Park to Camberwell, the West End, the City and further afield to the outskirts of Greater London, to Woking and Guildford. Here was my ideal document, an aide-mémoire of a semi-professional musician which in my hands would become a guidebook from which to uncover zones of urban erasure and survival in present-day London. The routes that I could plot using the diary might retrieve social histories previously lost within the constantly changing built environment.

This was my intention but as it transpires I did not do that. There were no walks from 23 Blandford Road where he lived to 42 Woodstock Road in Bedford Park where he moved to. There are no comparisons to be set side by side between Marylebone then and now. Instead, as I focused more and more on the content of the diary other patterns of interest began to emerge. I began to consider William Arthur as a kind of unselfconscious author, an individual engaged in an unconscious writing of his own very immediate history. Sometimes his text took the form of cryptic notes, and at other times William Arthur had decided to include fully formed sentences. The more I read the diary, the more I began to see it as a kind of autobiography and myself as a biographer. The entire concept of time and distance began to shift away from the geography of the capital to that of my own generational relation to William Arthur.

The diary is one cultural form which is open to novelisation[2] and increasingly to cinematic treatment. One way in which we make sense of who we are and where we want to be is through narrative. Diaries stabilise this process by constructing narrative connections which may be contingent upon the external world. Over time keeping a diary becomes a habit forming process involving a simple and effective means of constructing and reconstructing one's personality. It can be seen as a systematic and uncluttered approach to life which directly involves the subject as both reader and writer of his or her own life patterns. I approach my great-grandfather's diary as an autobiographical text which on close inspection opens up the psychological topographies of my own family history. It not only focuses other family stories locked within an archive of family heirlooms but also acts as an historical lens through which a particular domestic milieu can be viewed, in this case in the months preceding World War One. The pocket diary involves elements of autobiographical modelling and an attention to locality. These build into a complex web of evidence and narrations. In turn, Family History is brought into relation to what is conventionally considered to be the work of the professional historian.

I want to explore these concerns by looking at two areas. These micro and macro studies might then start to develop some of the historical work of recent years, like that of Carolyn Steedman and Angela V. John, to create new debates about public history and historiography.[3] Firstly I will look at *timewriting,* at the diary as an individual's approach to time at a localised level, and then at the process of *researching* – seeing the diary as a key to the exploration of ancestral time.

Timewriting
The diary and time
Within William Arthur's diary there are a number approaches to time. The pocket diary not only involved William Arthur in a process of 'backtelling',[4] whereby brief retrospective accounts of each day were jotted down, but perhaps more significantly for him it also operated as a tool for 'foretelling', a means of anticipating and plotting future appointments. It is this relationship between past and future which makes the diary such a rich source of private and, as I will discuss later, unselfconscious history writing. This tension between the two modes of 'timewriting' is amplified by the abruptness of the 'author's' death as recorded in the pocket book by the hand of his partner, Lydia.

In *The Birth of the Museum* Tony Bennett begins to approach the relationship between the physicality of the museum and the interpretative behaviour of the visitor/audience by resurrecting Thomas Huxley's notion of the 'backteller'. Huxley had been taken with Voltaire's character Zadig, who had the ability to 'visualise an animal from the tracks it had left behind'.[5] Huxley framed this idea as a process of 'retrospective prophecy' and explained what seemed contradictory at first glance, to be a notion of prophetic reasoning, resting on a system of procedures that could be applied either retrospectively or prospectively. He suggested that 'the essence of the prophetic operation ... does not lie in its backward or forward relation to the course of time, but in the fact that it is the apprehension of that which lies out of the sphere of immediate knowledge; the seeing of that which to the natural sense of the seer is invisible.'[6] 'Backtellers' then are retrospective prophets involved in the construction of narratives out of a trail of clues. The detective novel revolves explicitly around an illustration of backtelling in which the detective policeman discovers a burglar from the marks made by his shoe. In this way the detective story is governed by the art of backward construction. These narrative processes may also be central to all forms of historical work whether it be the forensic activities of a palaeontologist the practice of an archivist, the role of the curator or indeed the memory work of the auto/biographer.

The diary as past self
A conventional definition of a diary might be that of a day-to-day record of events, ranging from the personal to that of the public. It could be argued that a diary always involves the construction of another reader by the author. This 'other' may be consciously considered by the diarist as an external audience or wider readership, or developed at a psychological level via the construction of an additional 'self'. The latter may emerge at varying degrees of self-consciousness or may lie submerged within the confines of the unconscious. However it might not be possible to effectively distinguish between these two modes as they exist enmeshed in the territory between being and doing. Diaries have close links with the literary genre of autobiography and often play a significant part in the production of an author's life story.

William Arthur Jewson's retrospections involve only brief synopses of a day's events. For example on Saturday 3 January 1914 he writes: 'Fred[7] comes. Bought Gerald's[8] stamp album. To Union Park and dined at 'The Corner House'. Fred spent the evening with us and Ethel[9] called.' His diary is peppered with backward glances and brief summations. On the 19 January Lydia visited Ethel while William Arthur 'spent evening at Ritsons.[10] Went to Cinema Wonderland at Poly with her and had tea out. Gerald with Mary[11] to Seldons.' These notations are the kind of raw materials from which a conventional biography might draw and embellish upon.

The diary as time planner
The back pages of William Arthur's diary highlight a further disposition towards ordering by way of accounts and check lists. There is a sense that William Arthur uses his diary as a tool by which he models his daily life. This is very different to

my own practice. My own academic diary involves brief notes, mnemonic lists and 'hieroglyphics' to help me keep track of my schedules. It is a hardback document distressed and bulging with scraps of additional paper and notes and bears the marks of a range of pens and highlighters. In contrast William Arthur's pocket diary is less cryptic in its style and is uniform in its use of one single type of indelible pencil. In years to come my own diary will read like a fragmented text unlike that of William Arthur which still retains elements of illustrative narrative cohesion through his daily reflections. The combination of fragmented lists, visual codes and hurried notations that sustain the abundance of today's filofaxes, timetables, diaries, digital organisers and updates amounts to a shattering of previous conceptions of a located self through fully formed recollections. William Arthur's document is a portable record (albeit an inevitably edited version of his time) which indicates his expanding social network.

The diary as foretelling

William Arthur's diary demonstrates forward planning in the form of noted appointments. When William Arthur died on 26 April 1914 he had no less than twelve musical appointments pending. These spanned the following four weeks and included work with the Woking Musical Society, the London County Council's Choral Union and the London Orchestral Society.[12] The engagements are noted as abbreviations and are written in indelible pencil. The implication that music was central to William's life is strongly suggested, for if one were to remove these notes the diary would be empty save for the entries of Wednesday 6 May 1914, which reads: 'Gerald to Margate. 3.5 Victoria', and Sunday 17 May 1914, which states: 'Richards – Thew Church'. In addition there are retrospective glances within the diary, acknowledgements and summaries which briefly mark a realisation of his plans. Both forward planning and retrospection come together in the activity of keeping the diary; a process amounting to a present which continuously regulates the everyday:

The everyday is situated at the intersection of two modes of repetition: the cyclical, which dominates in nature, and the linear, which dominates in processes known as 'rational'. The everyday implies on the one hand cycles, nights and days, seasons and harvests, activity and rest, hunger and satisfaction, desire and fulfilment, life and death, and it implies on the other hand the repetitive gestures of work and consumption.¹³

The foretelling present in William Arthur's diary, then, operates as a form of life management.

A diary, that apparently most authentic and immediate of documents, is quite as subject as any other literary artifice, and as interesting to the historian – and perhaps, even more the psychoanalyst – for what it represses, as for what it says.'¹⁴

'L'
Although humble in appearance, the diary must have figured importantly in the Jewson household for when William Arthur died on the 26 April 1914 of a massive stroke, his partner Lydia entered the words 'Died at 5.30 – L' in large handwriting in the appropriate space.¹⁵ This stark intervention underlines the particular gender politics within the Jewson family and highlights another dimension, that of an intangible 'present' as represented by the finality and certainty of death.

Esther Lydia Furley (known as Lydia) was born in 1872. The daughter of a gold beater she grew up in London where she worked as a dressmaker. In 1896, at the age of 24, she was employed as a waitress in a tea shop. Here she met William Arthur Jewson, 'a gentleman of independent means', married but with no children. An affair blossomed and in 1897 Gerald Arthur Jewson was born out of wedlock to Lydia at her home of 32 Balmes Road, De Beauvoir Town, Hackney. Her artisan family had moved over generations from Commercial Road to the periphery of the East End. Subsequently the couple moved into William Arthur's home at 54 St. Charles' Square in North Kensington, a move which was to bring previously unattainable financial comforts to Esther Lydia Furley-Jewson and enabled her to pursue more fully her activities in the suffrage movement, arts and crafts, acting and theosophy.¹⁶ It was probably on moving to North Kensington that Lydia struck up what would become a lifelong friendship with Miss Nellie Limouzin, the young aunt of Eric Blair (George Orwell)¹⁷ who was also involved in the Actresses' Franchise League and who lived round the corner on Portobello Road. However, as my mother recalled, 'Esther Lydia wished to separate from William Arthur Jewson, possibly in 1912 or 1913 before his death in 1914 but he said they should remain together because of their son Gerald. Lydia was friendly with Mrs Emmeline Pankhurst (who was 8 to 10 years her senior) and very friendly with Nellie Limouzin, who in later life would stay with Esther at her home (known as The Kiln) in Wisborough Green, West Sussex. My mother also hinted that by 1914 relations between William Arthur and Lydia were distanced if not strained. William Arthur was sixteen years her senior. By 1914, when he was 58, his younger partner is said to have protested under her breath 'at the old man pawing at her.'

This family story may provide a clue as to why Lydia entered William Arthur's time of death in his diary. Throughout the diary her whereabouts were constantly noted. It becomes a lens through which we can plot her activities as a part-time art student at Camberwell Polytechnic on Tuesday evenings or as a politically minded individual attending suffrage meetings and demonstrations in Hyde Park. William Arthur often met Lydia after these activities and went to dinner at one of the many Lyons Corner Houses or to the cinema. Lydia's immediate relations (her sisters' families being the Ritsons and the Harsants) made frequent visits to the Jewson's house. Apparently she was never very far away from William Arthur's thoughts. Her insertion in the diary implied that she had finally arrived at a point where she could assert symbolic control of her life within the relationship. She could now write about him and his activities in the same place where her own behaviour had been monitored and controlled. Lydia's intervention constitutes reflective experience in its most powerful form. It registers William Arthur's death but also carries her own autobiographical presence through the briefest of signatures – 'L'.

Researching
Reading and writing
In the course of researching the lives of William Arthur and Lydia I visited the Family Records Centre in London, where the atmosphere is very different to other archives in the metropolis. The emphasis is not placed on the act of writing. Only a few desks are provided, located along the walls or in the odd alcove on the ground floor. In contrast the focus of activity revolves around the endless array of shelves which hold the large format registers within which lists of data are recorded.

It takes both hands to carry these heavy ledgers to the long lecturn-like reading benches which are positioned between the shelves. One hears a constant background murmur of voices in discussion. The dialogue I could overhear involved family stories or anecdotes which had been prompted by the visit or which were in the process of being verified or questioned. This exchange is not always confined to relations or 'colleagues', for strangers strike up conversation as and when interests coincide. All the research in the Family Records Centre is 'primary'. There are no secondary or tertiary texts being consulted. Everyone is engaged in unearthing specific names, places and dates from the same source. The popular conception of the Family History phenomenon might be that it is the marketed pastime of the elderly or retired, a section of the population obsessed with uncovering their own bloodlines in the vain hope that they will discover a royal or famous pedigree to their family name. This stereotype may be why the academy has never engaged with the phenomenon. Indeed, even what might be termed as the interdisciplinary or progressive factions of the historical community have to some extent failed to acknowledge genealogy's relevance.

The historian Eric Hobsbawm gave genealogy some thought in the 1990s. In *On History* he suggests, albeit sceptically, that the practice of genealogy has both disadvantages and potential for the study of the past. On the minus side he views genealogy as a consumerist cul-de-sac, '...that which seeks to buttress an uncertain self-esteem. Bourgeois parvenus seek pedigrees, new nations or movements annex examples of past greatness and achievement to their history in proportion as they feel their actual past to have been lacking in these things....'[18] This I feel is a rather limited view of genealogy, one which sees any extra-curricula sense of the past as a threat to the academy.[19] The question of Family History's scholarly authority was therefore in my mind when I visited the Family History Fair in May 1998. This two-day convention was organised by the Society of Genealogists and involved family history societies, computer software companies, archival and conservation organisations, microfilm and microfiche suppliers, tour operators, the Commonwealth War Graves Commission, postcard traders, printers, professional research organisations, publishers, booksellers, record offices and secondhand book dealers. In addition there were representatives from the British Records Association, the Federation of Family History Societies, Friends of The Public Records Office, the Institute of Heraldic and Genealogical Studies and the British Association for Local History.

Lineage and locality
As might be guessed from this list of exhibitors, the Fair inevitably fell into regional sections. This seemed to contradict the idea that Family History is merely a private investigation, opening it up to a broader social exploration. However, the image of the family historian as just another obsessive hobbyist or amateur collector of dead ancestors is, I would argue, a representation constructed not only from inside the academy but also one nurtured in part from within its own culture. Family History has 'in-house' rules that revolve around the production and consumption of family-tree charts and the protocols of buying certificates. The practice's mixture of the subjective and the scientific is exemplified in Mark Herber's *Ancestral Trails,* heralded at the Fair as the definitive book on the subject of genealogy.

Tracing your family history is... particularly suitable for those who enjoy historical detective work; sorting new information, analysing clues and deciding the next step to take. As with most research, luck also plays an important part... you may find it easy to trace many generations within a few hours if, for example, you find a register for a parish where your ancestors lived for centuries. If you find a link with a family that possessed a title or substantial property, one of the published works containing genealogies of the nobility or gentry will take you back several centuries. Such links are surprisingly common.[20]

The many family histories which I saw at the Genealogical Society's Fair were written in a particularly dry and 'logical' style and built from chronological segments. Despite the risk of becoming impenetrable to the reader this style of Family History gives an overall sense of a whole and seamless history. I embarked initially upon a similar project, beginning with what I thought to be a wide range of ingredients, a mix of information gleaned from the Family Records Centre, my own interpretation of William Arthur's diary and discussions with my mother Barbara Brennan (née Jewson, William Arthur's granddaughter). This enabled me to compile a conventional chronological 'life story' of my great-grandfather with speed and ease. One measure of the private importance of William

Arthur's diary may lie in its survival to the present day as part of an accumulative family archive of memorabilia. This collection maps a set of histories and family stories common to my maternal line. However, the process of 'doing' this family history uncovered discrepancies both in the family's stories and in official histories. Areas of narrative and factual disjuncture emerged. That which had seemed so solid over the years began quickly melting into air.

Gerald Jewson was Lydia's son, born at her parents' house at 52 Balmes Road, De Beauvoir Town, Hackney, on 1 July, 1897. However, where I expected to find his surname to be entered as Jewson I found Furley. Jewson was given to him *only* as a christian name. His full name appears as follows: *Gerald Arthur Jewson Furley*. Furthermore there is no mention of the father's name, no William Arthur; only a dash. (Esther) Lydia's occupation is given as dressmaker. William Arthur's will and codicil (1910 and 1912) explicitly bequeath money and goods to (Esther) Lydia Furley's son Gerald Arthur Jewson Furley. This is evidence that William Arthur never legally adopted Gerald and I know from my mother that Gerald never changed his name by deed-poll. Within this context Gerald Arthur Jewson may have been fathered by another man (although his father was *probably* William Arthur) and his marriage certificate to my grandmother Elsie Lovell is invalid, as he entered 'Jewson' as his surname. Likewise his death certificate is incorrect as it bears the same discrepancy. Information of this kind tests the concept of family. Whether William Arthur was Gerald's real father or not does not alter the fact that the Jewson, Furley association took the form of a mutually contracted unit. However, what is problematised is the underpinning of the notion of a family's validity by a deep rooted and identifiable ancestral pool.

William Arthur's diary and its accompanying family history are significant in the way they depict the development of a particular musical way of life before the First World War. The family's involvement in the production, presentation and teaching of music displays an obvious transition from that of the aristocratic conventions at the height of the British Empire to that of a metropolitan and modernist culture. This is most striking in William Arthur's involvement in the London County Council Choral Union, the musical wing of an increasingly liberal minded, centralised administration committed to providing amenities for the expanding population of London after 1889.[21] William Arthur translated the accrued knowledge and experience which his family had gained amongst aristocratic circles over the preceding century to circumvent his father's prohibition on himself and his brothers pursuing careers as professional musicians and construct a semi-professional network of activities embedded within the emerging culture and 'civil service' of London.

Locality might be important for those studying social groups bound to one place of work with low pay and little or no prospect of escape. But for the middle-class gentleman of independent means like William Arthur, the politics of time, place and economy are of secondary importance. In contrast they are replaced by the ability and the possibility to travel with ideas, to transgress the bounds of local history and fixed notions of community to play out concerns within broader contexts. In this sense it is interesting to refer back to William Arthur's diary to see what is *not* there. It does not give us a sense of current affairs. There is mention of the deportation of South African Labour (Party) members on 27 February 1914 and the ensuing Hyde Park demonstration on 1 March, but there are no references to daily news items such as the uniting of Northern and Southern Nigeria, the murder of Gaston Calmette by Mme. Caillaux, the Bank of England's authorisation by government to issue money in excess of the statutory limit, Shackleton's leading of the Antarctic expedition, or the opening of the Panama Canal. Neither does he speak of musical developments such as the first performance of Vaughan Williams' 'A London Symphony', or Rutland Boughton's Glastonbury opera, 'The Immortal Hour'. These omissions are, of course, nothing out of the ordinary in an appointments book or pocket memo. Instead of current affairs William Arthur's diary briefly traces the process of buying a new house, comments upon visitors, notes his partner's appointments and keeps track on his sons' whereabouts and activities. The pocket book acts as a guide to everyday life.

Family history

At present Family History lies on the threshold of the academy, its nearest academic equivalents being Sociology, and aspects of Cultural Studies such as those analyses in the 1960s and 1970s of the extended and nuclear family within kinship networks. It is possible that it may in time more fully enter academic discourse. There are already courses emerging out of the Open University's work on 'Time, Family and Community: Perspectives on Family History and Community History'.[22] A major appeal of genealogy and family history may be that it provides people with a sense of continuity and of belonging. As new evidence is uncovered by the family historian a sense of security and identity may well unfold. Simple forms of data like the date of a birth, the cause of a death, or the address of an individual seem to 'fix' a past existence and verify or explode well furrowed mythologies. Experience is often mundane in nature and not punctuated with important achievements. In this context Family History may be seen as the antithesis of both autobiography and biography; genres which tend to document great deeds. Dates of births, deaths and marriages, census returns, heirlooms and memories combine as a narrative machinery which is used by the family historian to construct a notion of 'self '. 'This also suggests a rejection of conventional cultural institutions as the sole arbiters of legitimacy and value.'[23]

I can identify a number of motivations and stages which emerge over a sustained period of Family History research like those carried out by my mother or myself. Initially there is often a genuine interest in discovering and charting bloodlines. This loses its appeal once a substantial genealogy has been constructed. This genealogy, consisting of chronologies, lists of ancestors and family trees might then be used to validate, question and test family stories and mythologies seemingly ingrained as truth through repetition. Broader contextual work might be developed in the form of social vignettes or local histories, which in turn give way to the exploration of the ways of life or ideas and cultural practices which may have been rooted within the family across generations. In time the researcher might experience the procedure as a therapeutic or psychological process focused on the retrieval and portrayal of the dead. Past names become fully rounded people, a stage which is linked closely to the initial motivation but differing in its understanding that ancestral ties are common to us all and not dependent on assumptions of pedigree or lineage. This stage operates as a kind of *memento mori* for the living researcher as she/he manoeuvres through the community of the dead.

Modernist views of an unfolding historical process are jettisoned in favour of a more internalised and intersubjective invention of the past. This interpretation of past is not necessarily regarded as full blown history. The 'pasts' in question exist on a much smaller scale to those of Hobsbawm's aerial view or the kind of central story as posed (and opposed) by Caroline Steedman. In the current general political environment there is not much interest in the past. The traditional Left has shifted from ideological accounts to that of the autobiographical or self-studies. However, Family History has a language and codification of its own. There is ritual involved in its process. Among the discussions at the Family Records Centre or in the pages of *Family History Magazine* there is the implication that material will be shared. Notices are placed regarding family names and genealogical lines of inquiry, and these draw responses. Attraction to the area might revolve around the idea of uncovering blood-ties, but after this initial right of passage a richer and broader sense of relationships emerges, one whose constituency is based on a valuing of data uncovered. Family History and its more formal cousin genealogy may then be seen as democratic scholarship that lies outside the academy as process.

Notes

1. Gerald Arthur Jewson (1897-1980) was William Arthur's only surviving child born to Lydia. In 1914 at the age of seventeen he was a boarding pupil at Margate College in Kent and the diary is consistently punctuated with references to Gerald's visits back home at weekends and during holiday periods.
2. Michail Bakhtin, 'Epic and Novel' *The Dialogic Imagination: Four Essays*, trans. Carly Emerson and Michael Holquist, Texas University Press, 1981, pp. 15, 7, 30.
3. Angela V. John, *Elizabeth Robins: Staging a Life*, 1862–1952, Routledge, London, 1995. Carolyn Steedman, 'History and Autobiography', *Past Tenses*, Rivers Oram Press, London, 1992. Tim Brennan *Notes From The Edge*, MA Public History & Historiography dissertation, Ruskin College, Oxford, 1998.
4. Tony Bennett, *The Birth of the Museum*, Routledge, London, 1995, pp. 177–181.
5. Ibid, pp. 177–181.
6. Ibid, pp. 177–181. As Bennett then suggests, the only aspect which alters within this prophetic process is 'the relation to time'. p. 178.
7. A friend of William Arthur Jewson's son Gerald Arthur Jewson.
8. Gerald Arthur Jewson was sixteen years old in 1914. He was the only child of William Arthur Jewson and Esther Lydia Furley.
9. Ethel Harsant was Esther Lydia Furley's sister.
10. Florence Eliza Ritson was Esther Lydia Furley's sister.
11. Mary Davis was a long standing family servant.
12. For more on the politics of the London County Council see Susan D.

Pennybacker, *A Vision of London 1889-1914: Labour, Everyday Life and the LCC Experiment*, Routledge, London, 1995.

13 Henri Lefebvre, 'The Everyday and Everydayness', in *Yale French Studies 73*, Yale, 1987, p. 10.
14 Raphael Samuel 'Fragment From A Diary 1968', *History Workshop Journal* 1967–91, Oxford, p. 7.
15 William and Lydia were common law man and wife. On 30 April, 1879 William Arthur Jewson had married his first cousin Frederica Blanche Ashton in the parish church of St. Marylebone in London. For whatever reasons by the early 1890s their marriage had become irretrievable. Around 1894-96 William Arthur begins a relationship with Esther Lydia Furley (Lydia). The two never married but Lydia was known as a Mrs Jewson and their son as Gerald Furley Jewson.
16 Lydia was arrested for chaining herself to the gates of Buckingham Palace, was a part-time student at Camberwell Polytechnic and later in life had a relationship with M.P Shiel, a theosophist writer and friend of W.T. Stead.
17 In the 1930s Miss Limouzin had an apartment in Paris. She was the 'favourite aunt' on whom Eric Blair would rely when experiencing difficulties with writing *Down and Out in Paris and London*. See Dervla Murphy's introduction to *George Orwell Down and Out in Paris and London*, 1933, Penguin edition 1989, London, pp. viii–ix.
18 Eric Hobsbawm, *On History*, Weidenfeld and Nicholson, London, 1997, p. 21.
19 However, Hobsbawm does recognise that over the past few generations history as a discipline has broadened beyond what he calls the 'academic canoe'. Ibid, pp. 59–60.
20 Mark D. Herber *Ancestral Trails – The Complete Guide to British Genealogy and Family History*, Sutton Publishing, Stroud, 1997, p. xiii.
21 From 'The Expansion of London 1918-39: Topographies and Mentalities' a seminar given by Sally Alexander (27 May 1998) as part of the series: 'Researching the Metropolis' organised by Raphael Samuel Centre for the Study For Metropolitan Cultural History, Bishopsgate Institute and University of East London.
22 See Michael Drake (ed.), *Time, Family and Community: Perspectives on Family History and Community History*, The Open University, Blackwell Publishers, London, 1994.
23 Thanks to Paul Martin for these thoughts, Ruskin College Oxford, 1998.

Save 'our' red squirrel: kill the American grey tree rat

An exploration of the role of the red and the grey squirrel in constructing ideas of Englishness

Hilda Kean

The red squirrel currently occupies a special place in England's heritage. Yet it is present almost entirely as an image, commonly seen as an icon of a mythic countryside past on Christmas cards or adorning the television advertisements of NPI, a pension specialist, with its bright red tail and careful hoarding of nuts. Although NPI was established in 1835, at a time when red squirrels were common in England and Wales, the squirrel logo was not introduced until the early 1960s and at that time was blue in colour. Only in 1994 did the company introduce the red squirrel into its advertisements, using pictures of red squirrels from the National Trust reserve in Formby.[1] While the firm has sponsored conservation projects designed to maintain the remaining red squirrel colonies in Cumbria, it has also initiated annual national heritage awards.[2] Visitors to historic properties are invited to nominate their favourite property, and best gift shop, on leaflets sporting these charming red creatures; the winners are rewarded with an antiques voucher.[3] For the NPI this strategy has apparently worked well. Fifty-five percent of people surveyed during 1999 recognised the red squirrel logo as that of NPI. Moreover, the linking of the red squirrel with specific heritage sponsorship drew in the desired target groups: the AB and C1s.[4]

The red squirrel: image and reality

Although we may readily recognise the red squirrel image, an advertisement or heritage award leaflet is the nearest most of us in England will ever come to actually seeing such a creature. Currently the only places where wild red squirrels are likely to be found in England are the Isle of Wight, Brownsea Island in Dorset , parts of the north east and north west and parts of East Anglia.[5] Their rarity is a relatively new phenomenon. As early as 1840 red squirrels were widespread, but liable to destroy young trees and so subject to summary shooting.[6] Before the Great War the red squirrel was so abundant and so destructive in some areas , particularly the Scottish Highlands and Cornwall, that shooting clubs were formed to kill them.[7] Indeed the prolific Highland red squirrel was so little regarded as worth preserving that it was recommended as a tasty wartime dish with 'an ineradicable "piney" flavour' drawn from its diet of conifers'.[8]

However, by the 1920s there was growing concern about the disappearance of the red squirrel in the wild,[9] its possible loss discussed in the scientific press and in magazines like *Country Life* and *The Field*. But it is only in the last 20 years that the red squirrel has become consolidated as a motif of England's heritage. At a time when the red squirrel could no longer be experienced as a living part of the actually existing countryside it became a symbol in the representation of a particular idea of English as a nation.[10] The National Heritage Act 1980 was designed to preserve a range of properties and to seek some sort of public access for cultural consumption. As Patrick Wright has argued, it was also intended to ensure that 'heritage' was displayed as such.[11] The red squirrel, I want to suggest, has become iconic of the nation alongside such symbols of Englishness as red phone boxes, warm beer and cricket bats. While it was the 1930s which saw the origins of the construction of the red squirrel as an indigenous creature threatened by a foreign menace, it was in the more recent past that this 'sleeping image' was resurrected as a symbol of tradition and nationality.[12]

At the same time as the red squirrel has been disappearing from the English countryside it has made its entry into the world of heritage stamps, Tufty Clubs, stuffed displays in provincial museums and sponsorship of heritage competitions. In the Jubilee year 1977 postage stamps of five British wild animals painted by Patrick Oxenham were issued to show examples of threatened wildlife: the hedgehog, hare, otter, badger and red squirrel.[13] Concurrently the red squirrel was

1977 postage stamp featuring a red squirrel

receiving a different sort of recognition, promoted by the Royal Society for the Prevention of Accidents. The animal transmogrified into Tufty, a benign and decorously clothed red squirrel intended to instruct small children and their parents in correct traffic behaviour. By 1978 nearly 22,000 Tufty Clubs were running.[14] Instruction notes and special songs were circulated through a national network. Tufty was seen as an animal with whom children could identify, and who would behave sensibly. Reflecting on the popularity of Tufty, the Royal Society for the Prevention of Accidents (RoSPA) has recently suggested this was in large part due to the fact that children liked him and learnt about safety in a non-threatening way.[15] The increasing visibility of the red squirrel as a benign character – rather than a destroyer of Highland timber – and as an emblem of a mythic past has developed side by side with its disappearance from the natural environment.

The friendly grey squirrel or marauding American tree rat

My consideration so far of the physical demise and re-created presence of the red squirrel has been presented somewhat unproblematically. However, the demise of the red squirrel is linked frequently, but incorrectly, to the spread of the grey squirrel. And the grey squirrel is depicted as distinctive not because of its different colourings (it is often brown with reddish patches at certain times of the year) but because it is a 'foreign', non-indigenous mammal, often referred to scathingly as an American tree rat.

Although grey squirrels were present in England and Wales from 1830, their spread is usually attributed to the whims of various aristocrats releasing what were domestic pets into the wild.[16] Indeed, so concerned was A. D. Middleton about the increase of grey squirrels in England and Wales that he catalogued over 32 separate releases of squirrels into the countryside from 1876 to 1929.[17] Of particular importance to him was the foreign origin of the squirrel:

I know of more than one patriotic Englishman who has been embittered against the whole American nation on account of the presence of their squirrels in his garden.[18]

However, the grey squirrels also became very popular because of their perceived friendliness and alertness. They rapidly became favourites with visitors to London parks. The grey squirrels in Regent's Park, for example, had originated from those released from the Zoo where they had been placed by the Duke of Bedford.[19] In this respect park administrators were emulating the American practice: squirrels had been introduced into Central Park in New York and so enjoyed their habitat that they proliferated.[20] By 1922 the British government was considering introducing bird sanctuaries in London's royal parks and recognised the potential conflict of interest between rare birds and marauding squirrels. Eradication of the squirrels, however, was rejected outright as an option because of public opinion in their favour.[21]

The spread of the grey squirrel in the 1920s, particularly in London and the Home Counties coincided with a severe decline in the red squirrel population. The question whether there was a causal relationship between these two events troubled scientists and professional 'countrymen'. Scientists tended to view such a relationship sceptically: the red squirrel population had declined because of proclivity to certain diseases.[22] 'Countrymen' were less considered in their approach. As one declared, 'I am of the opinion that such a deplorable state of affairs [demise of the red] is entirely due to the importation of the American grey squirrel.'[23] Less restrained was the robust assertion:

This alien enemy [the grey squirrel] is said to be spreading fast throughout parts of the Home Counties, where, like all aliens it is rapidly dispossessing the native squirrel. [24]

By 1931 public concern about the possible demise of the red squirrel and the responsibility of the foreign grey for this deplorable state of affairs, which took scant note of scientists' opinions, was at its height. This was a particular obsession of contributors to *Country Life* and *The Field* who wrote enthusiastically to the magazines on the extent of the perceived problem. As the caption under the photograph of a grey squirrel, in a leading article published in *Country Life* in May 1931, characterised it, this squirrel was the 'prisoner at the bar'.[25]

The squirrel and the nation in 1930s England

Why did concern peak at this time although no new sitings of grey squirrel colonies were reported then by scientists? As I have argued elsewhere, to understand why certain animals become popular or are seen as worthy of particular defence and protection (or vilification) at certain times owes less to the behaviour of the animals and more to broader political, social and cultural concerns in human society.[26]

In the 1920s and 1930s both left and right focused on the nature of land and the countryside. While the 1926 speech 'On England' of the Conservative Prime Minister Stanley Baldwin has become almost a cliché through over-quotation it is worth reiterating his organising conceit, namely, ' To me, England is the country, and the country is England.'[27] Such a rural idyll became a 'key means of representing the nation'.[28] In different ways progressives and reactionaries alike were engaged in constructing ideas of Englishness in which notions of land, landscape, and country were central. This period saw the establishment and growth of what became the League Against Cruel Sports,[29] and, to counter its campaigns, the British Field Sports Society.[30] The Ramblers' Association and British Workers' Sports Federation, set up to challenge the privatisation of land and exclusion of walkers from the wild, were also created at this time.[31] In different vein Harold John Massingham, the forerunner of the modern ecological movement,[32] looked to organic farming and the benign treatment of animals to create a new way of life.[33] For Massingham it was to the countryside that England had to look to find and consolidate its roots.[34]

Such views of Englishness and a return to the land were not confined to the left. Many English countryside enthusiasts turned to Nazi Germany for inspiration.[35] As E.D. Randall, the fascist poet , declared, people should 'leave the unreality of the cities for the reality of cosmic harmony...to return to the life of the soil and sun'.[36] Henry Williamson, better known as the author of *Tarka the Otter* than for his fascism, made his own turn to the land in the 1930s, working a farm in Norfolk. This was in response to the system which he proclaimed was, 'made by townsmen, which cared little or nothing for the soil and the people. A nation that neglected its soil, neglected its soul; and its people would perish.'[37] In more nuanced fashion the same sentiment is expressed in *Tarka the Otter,* his book proselytising against the then still legal and barbaric 'sport' of otter hunting. Here Williamson looked to the landowners to defend the countryside against farmers who would exterminate nearly every wild bird and animal.[38] It is in the context of this contest for definition of the countryside within broader political cultures that the 'battle' between the grey and red squirrel took place. While the red squirrel, despite its acknowledged delinquency as a destroyer of trees, was constructed as an established symbol of an idyllic rural Britain, the grey squirrel was frowned upon for being an alien despoiler of indigenous culture and for the favour it found with those seen as anathema to the countryside – people who lived in towns, or *horribile dictu*, the suburbs.

The dancing defiance of the tree rat or the welcome garden visitor

A. D. Middleton, who carried out his research on the grey squirrel with a grant from the Empire Marketing Board, wrote widely on the problem in language designed to create fear of the unknown:

> The importance of adopting a definitely inimical attitude towards grey squirrels cannot be over-emphasized, for there is every reason to believe that these aliens will quickly become an unmitigated pest of a hitherto unknown character throughout the country.[39]

For Middleton one problem, as the government had previously recognised, was that grey squirrels were popular in towns. As he put it, they were 'ideal "park animals"', but outside their native country there was 'no limit to [their] depredations'.[40]

The debate reached a climax in the first months of 1931, with heated exchanges in *The Field* and *Country Life*, questions in parliament and a Ministry of Agriculture conference designed to tackle the problem. Dramatic language was employed on all sides. As one explained, although the grey squirrel might cause damage in the country, ' as yet, no one has complained of any serious outrage by him in London'. The grey squirrel in her own garden was 'a welcome visitor, and I should regret to see him murdered'.[41] Another sympathetic gardener from Buckinghamshire left nuts for the grey squirrel on his bird table and admired his character, ' He is supremely indifferent to the presence of three or four dogs and an Atco mowing machine.'[42] Indeed it was the very presence of grey squirrels in towns which led, some argued, to their endorsement by those possessing that apparent city characteristic of sentiment. Bournemouth, one declared, was being overrun and the squirrel was 'regarded with favour by occupants of perambulators and by dear old ladies of both sexes.'[43] A hostile correspondent from Surrey recounted seeing a group of six grey squirrels being admired by a crowd in London's Russell Square. 'When I ventured to suggest that I should kill [them] with my stick the whole crowd seemed horrified.' The public, he went on, should be taught that the squirrels were, in fact, rats.[44] Those working in the countryside were less than enchanted by squirrel antics, 'These squirrel rats are everywhere and for every one shot there are 50 dancing defiance on the tree tops; skipping along fences or camouflaging themselves where nobody can see them.'[45] These foreign hordes were castigated for such crimes as attacking pheasant chicks, chewing up celandines and eating – precisely – 174 young shoots and 252 cones from one fir tree.[46]

But there was not just the problem of the destruction of livelihood or gardens; the spread of the grey squirrel was seen as a threat to the indigenous red squirrel and the mythical way of life it represented. As a leading article in *The Field* suggested, 'We are confronted today, in short, with the opening stages of a plague ... In a short time the whole face of England will have been invaded by a foreign rodent which is omnivorous.'[47] Farmers concerned with the dumping of foreign sludge in British jams, vegetable imports which undermined the home market or the need for preferential tariffs within the Empire, identified with the red squirrel and saw the grey squirrel as a metaphor of foreign destruction.[48] There was consternation that grey squirrels physically drove out the reds, 'I have myself seen a grey squirrel chasing a red one from tree to tree, the unfortunate victim screaming with terror.'[49] Even worse, cross mating was feared.[50] In summary, the grey squirrel , as a *Field* editorial argued, was an enemy alike of the farmer, the fruit grower, the naturalist and the lover of English birds.[51] Those who sought to kill the squirrels with a greater vigour than in the past were not just defending their livelihoods but a particular idea of Englishness and establishing *who* had a right to defend that idea.

The question was raised in Parliament, particularly in the form of parliamentary questions to the Minister of Agriculture, Dr Addison. He was faced with the problem of MPs such as Samuel Rosbotham, Labour MP for Ormskirk, demanding that these American creatures be killed while balancing the concerns of other MPs that grey squirrels in public parks be maintained.[52] In response a conference on the problem of the grey squirrel was held in May 1931, attended by representatives of farming interests and rural local authorities, and by those concerned with the preservation and creation of heritage, such as the National Trust and Royal Society for the Protection of Birds. The conference brought together those defending a particular sort of English land literally and metaphorically.[53] A key participant was the newly formed National Anti-Grey Squirrel Campaign. This pressure group had been set up under the aegis of *The Field,* which was vehement about the threat of the squirrel. The grey squirrel was defamed as 'the worst menace with which our countryside has ever been threatened'. Even more hysterically the magazine suggested, 'In a short time the whole face of England will have been invaded by a foreign rodent which is omnivorous.'[54] The National Anti-Grey Squirrel Campaign run by L.Swainson from his home in Boxmoor in Hertfordshire was intended if not to exterminate the squirrels then to reduce them to a vanishing point.

Naturally *The Field* was delighted with the government conference on grey squirrels, attributing the event to the work of the magazine itself in raising the issue and helping to form the campaign.[56] While some suggested the introduction of particular traps, recipes for grey squirrel pies [57] or 'early rising and a gun',[58] the government confined its immediate activities to issuing an advisory leaflet through the Ministry of Agriculture.[59] While stating that , 'if the animal continues to be tolerated, and even encouraged, by a large number of people, as it certainly is at present, its increase can never be checked', the Ministry nevertheless felt it necessary to describe the grey squirrel – prominent eyes and rather small ears – as if its appearance was not widely known. It advised killing the first squirrels which migrated into an area by shooting or trapping and forming squirrel clubs or 'general vermin clubs' by landowners and farmers.[60] But this view was not hegemonic. Significantly, although legislation was introduced in 1931 against destructive 'non-indigenous animals' the creature which bore the brunt of the law was not the grey squirrel but the muskrat.[61]

By the 1950s the fear of the invading animal was heightened. Farmers illicitly introduced myxomatosis from Australia to destroy rabbits and formed themselves into rabbit clearance societies.[62] The 1954 Pests Act was introduced to assist rabbit destruction at the same time as the deliberate introduction of disease was outlawed in response to public outrage. While the government eventually took a calm line about the threat of rabbits, it showed no such restraint on the behaviour of the grey squirrel. Reissuing its earlier advice leaflet in a revised form in 1954, the Ministry of Agriculture and Fisheries expressed its grave concern in language which inflamed fear of foreign invasion. Although the grey squirrel had been regarded first as a pleasing addition to the fauna, it was now regarded as ' a most undesirable pest'. The foreign grey squirrel had invaded England: 'Every English county... has been entered'.

It 'invades country;' it 'will fell standing corn'; in fruit areas ' it will eat fruit'; it is a 'frequent robber of birds' nests, taking both eggs and chicks'. English animals – pheasants, partridges and poultry – were declared to be its 'victims'. In response farmers were advised to always 'carry a gun through squirrel infested land' (sic). This havoc was wreaked by a non-native animal and a half-breed at that – 'an intermediate between two sub species'. Amidst this otherwise alarming rhetoric the Ministry did accept that the considerable fluctuations in numbers of red squirrels were probably caused by disease, its suggestion that 'wherever [the grey squirrel] invades country inhabited by the red squirrel the latter eventually disappears' was not designed to reassure those interested in the conservation of the indigenous animal.[63] Certainly, at the end of the Second World War the red squirrel was more widely distributed than the grey: but by the 1970s the grey squirrels occupied almost four times more areas in England and Wales than the red.[64]

The English red squirrel now and the Scottish wild cat

As Raphael Samuel suggested, the last thirty years have witnessed an extraordinary and ever-growing enthusiasm for the recovery of the national past.[65] And it is within this context that, in England at least, the red squirrel has achieved a new lease of life as a symbol of a past. In Scotland the situation is somewhat different. The Royal Zoological Society of Scotland in its Highland Wildlife Park in Kingussie in Inverness-shire rears and releases abandoned and orphaned red squirrels taken in from all over Scotland.[66] Tourist postcards of Scottish wildlife do sometimes include the red squirrel. But the red squirrel does not perform the function of a creature which evokes a particular pastness in the way its English counterpart does. That function, I would suggest, is performed by the Scottish wild cat.

Looking rather like a bruiser tabby, the wild cat – not to be confused with a feral cat – is virtually extinct and protected by law. Competing with feral cats for food and territory the wild cat is increasingly unseen except on postcards of Scottish wildlife or stuffed and encased in the Inverness museum. Because the cat appears to look like its commonplace peers but is in fact rare it confounds us. What seems familiar but in fact is not, is thus conceived as exotic. In the same way that the colour and size of many grey squirrels invite comparisons with the red, in Scotland the distinction between rare wild cats and stray moggies is elided. Farmers are legally permitted to shoot marauding mogs, but pilfering wild cats are protected. As the images on the tourist postcards suggest, there is an exciting ambiguity about what is and what might be – the exotic in the back garden?[67] The exotic other could be mistaken by us for a stray mog. The very wildness is the attraction in these post-Braveheart days.[68]

In some ways the red squirrel is better known now than when it was widespread, for it was a shy animal veering away from crowds, hibernating in winter, and seeking refuge in forests away from built-up areas and thus rarely seen. Dunwich in Suffolk is a place where the live red squirrel is never seen. Like the town itself it has vanished. Once a thriving medieval religious and wool centre the now tiny village is better known today for its fish and chip shop on the shingle and the way it embodies transience as the North Sea continues to erode the land's defences.[69] The present itself is fragile, the past more so and thus merits preservation. In the last year of the twentieth century in the natural landscape section of the award winning Dunwich Museum is a stuffed red squirrel. The accompanying caption declares, ' it may have vanished as a result of being pushed out by the grey squirrel.'[70] The red squirrel's stuffed presence suggests a greater degree of permanence than the physical existence of the place where it is displayed. It suggests a past separate from the fragile present: like the squirrel the village itself can entirely disappear.

Ironically, in the 1980s when it was being appropriated as a symbol of English heritage some scientists suggested that the red squirrel might not even be British since its physical characteristics were not unique.[71] Whether this is true or not, the red squirrel can certainly be said to have established itself in the popular imagination of heritage, if not in the English countryside itself. Indeed, through its visual depiction it has been constructed as a tenacious creature holding on despite the odds. In this sense is has certainly become an English icon exhibiting the Dunkirk and Blitz spirit of resilience against the odds.[72] Certainly the red squirrel has an assured place in the emotions of the English irrespective of the actual existence of the grey squirrel. This owes less to its physical presence than to the rhetoric of its defenders some half-century ago.

Notes

I would like to thank the archive and public relations staff at the Royal Society for the Prevention of Accidents, Post Office Heritage and NPI, and the librarian of official papers in the Bodleian Library Lower Camera.

1. Correspondence from Sponsorship Manager NPI July 1999.
2. 'You can help red squirrels' NPI Red Alert North West. The Red Squirrel Conservation Partnership.
3. NPI National Heritage Awards Leaflet, 1999.
4. Correspondence from Sponsorship Manager NPI, July 1999.
5. H. G. Lloyd 'Past and Present Distribution of Red and Grey Squirrels', *Mammal Review*, vol 13 nos 2/3/4 1983, pp. 69 – 80; John Gurnell, *The Natural History of Squirrels*, 1987 p. 161; 'The Red Squirrel', Joint Nature Conservation Committee and NPI ,1998.
6. See George Waring, *The Squirrels and Other Animals* , London,1840, a collection of stories for children in which it is suggested that red squirrels should not be shot. 'The pleasure they afford us by exhibiting their wonderful leaps and feats of agility among the summer branches, more than repay us for their very trifling thefts.' p. 7.
7. Gurnell, *Natural History of Squirrels*, p. 162.
8. L. C .R. Cameron, *The Wild Foods of Great Britain*, Routledge,London, 1917.
9. Cpt C. W. R. Knight, *Wild Life in the Tree Tops*, Thornton Butterworth, London,1921, pp. 49–50; Gurnell, *The Natural History of Squirrels* , p. 162.
10. See David Boswell and Jessica Evans (eds.), *Representing the Nation: A Reader. Histories, Heritage and Museums,* Routledge, London, 1999.
11. Patrick Wright, *On Living in an Old Country,* London Verso 1985. Extract printed in Boswell and Evans *Representing the Nation,* p. 121. See also Robert Hewison, *Culture and Consensus. England, Art and Politics since 1940,* Methuen, London, 1997.
12. Raphael Samuel, Introduction: 'Exciting to be English' in Raphael Samuel (ed.) *Patriotism: The Making and Unmaking of British National Identity,* vol 1. Routledge, London, 1989 p. xxxi.
13. David Black, 'British Wildlife', *British Philatelic Bulletin*,Vol 15 no 2 October 1977, pp. 13–14.
14. 'Tufty Club Introduction notes. Suggested Guidelines for Tufty Club Leaders,' RoSPA, 1978, p. 1.
15. 'All our Yesterdays Look back in d-anger: The Tufty Years', *Safety Education*, RoSPA Summer 1999, p. 19
16. The Duke of Bedford who was responsible for releasing grey squirrels into Woburn Park is seen as a particular culprit. A. D. Middleton, *The Grey Squirrel*, Sidgwick & Jackson, London, 1931, pp. 14–21.
17. A. D. Middleton,*The Grey Squirrel*, 1931 p. 22. See too Hugh Boyd Watt, ' On the American Grey Squirrel in the British Isles', *The Essex Naturalist,* vol 20 1923, pp. 189–205.
18. A .D. Middleton, *The Grey Squirrel*, 1931, p. 1.
19. See too Boyd Watt, ' On the American Grey Squirrel ', *The Essex Naturalist*, vol 20 1923, p. 192.
20. Ernest T. Seton, ' Migration of the Gray Squirrel,' *Journal of Mammalogy* ,vol 1:2 February 1920, p. 56.
21. Ministry of Works Committee on Bird Sanctuaries in Royal Parks, *Bird Sanctuaries in Royal Parks,* HMSO, London, 1922, p. 5.
22. Middleton, *The Grey Squirrel,* p. 75; Gurnell, *Natural History*, p. 162; I.F.

Keyner, 'Diseases of Squirrels in Britain', *Mammal Review,* vol 13 nos 2/3/4/ 1983, p. 155; Lloyd, 'Past and Present Distribution', p. 69; Boyd Watt, *On the American Grey Squirrel,* p. 203.

23 Knight, *Wild Life in the Tree Tops,* p. 50.
24 Cameron,*Wild Foods of Great Britain,* p. 21.
25 'The Grey Squirrel', *Country Life* , 23 May 1931, p. xlviii.
26 Hilda Kean, *Animal Rights. Political and Social Change in Britain since 1800*, Reaktion Books ,London,1998.
27 He does not mention squirrels- of any sort – in his lyrical nostalgia The only animals mentioned are horses taking home hay to the farm at twilight.Stanley Baldwin, 'On England' in Stanley Baldwin, *On England*, Philip Allan, London 1926, pp. 6–7.
28 Sophie Breese, 'In Search of Englishness; in Search of Votes' in John Arnold, Kate Davies and Simon Ditchfield (eds.), *History and Heritage,* Donhead, Shaftesbury,1998, p. 156.
29 Kean, *Animal Rights*, p. 185–6.
30 Letter from James Fitzwilliam, *The Field*, 4 July 1931; *Cruel Sports* vol IV:9 September 1930, p. 73, which declared that the attempt to form the BFSS 'proves that at least we have driven our opponents out into the open'.
32 Ibid p. 187. See too Tom Stephenson, *Forbidden Land. The Struggle for Access to Mountain and Moorland*, Manchester University Press, Manchester 1989; Benny Rothman, *The 1932 Kinder Trespass* ,Willow Publishing, Altrincham, 1982. See also Lindsey Porter, *On Spartan Lines. Early Years of the YHA*, Ashbourne Editions, Ashbourne, n.d. (1992?).
32 David Wilkinson, 'Pioneering Champion of Ecology: The Life and Work of H.J. Massingham (1888-1952)' *Country Life*, August 18,1977; Edward Abelson (ed.), *A Mirror of England. An Anthology of the Writings of H J Massingham*, Green Books, Devon, 1988.
33 Edward Abelson (ed.) *A Mirror of England*.
34 H.J. Massingham (ed.), *The English Countryside* ,1939, p. 87. See too H.J. Massingham, *A Mirror of England*, pp. 68–69; *Country Relics,* CUP, Cambridge, 1939, p. 202. See Anna Bramwell, *Ecology in the Twentieth Century*, Yale University Press ,1989, pp. 125–130. For a discussion of Massingham's idea of Englishness in relation to craft,see Hilda Kean, 'East End Stories: The Chairs and the Photographs' in *International Journal of Heritage Studies* (forthcoming 2000).
35 Patrick Wright, *The Village That Died for England.The Strange Story of Tyneham*, London,1996, pp. 150–194; Bramwell, *Ecology in the Twentieth Century.*
36 As quoted in Philip Coupland, 'The Blackshirted Utopians', *Journal of Contemporary History* 33: 2 April 1998, p. 266.
37 Henry Williamson, *The Story of a Norfolk Farm*, 1941, p. 186–7
38 Henry Williamson, *Tarka the Otter*, (1927). Penguin Country Library edition, Harmondsworth, 1985, p. 103.
39 A.D. Middleton, 'The Grey Squirrel in the British Isles', *Journal of the Ministry of Agriculture*,vol xxxvii no 11 February 1931, p. 1078.
40 A.D.Middleton, 'The Grey Squirrel,' *Empire Forestry Journal* vol 10, 1931, p.15.
41 Letter from Dora Greville, *Country Life*, 2 January 1932, p. 27.
42 Letter from G McK. Bucks, *The Field*, 3 January 1931, p. 18.
43 Editorial article *The Field,* 28 March 1931, p. 420.
44 Letter from D.W.Laker, Coulsdon, Surrey, *The Field*, 20 June 1931, p. 901.
45 Letter from Wentworth, Crawley, *The Field*, 23 May 1931, p. 745.

46 Letter from John Balden, Bretton, Wakefield, *The Field*, 21 March 1931 p. 398; Letter from J C Handcross, Hampstead Heath, *The Field*, 18 April 1931, p. 551; Letter from A.J. Smith ,Hertford, *The Field*, 25 April 1931, p. 587.
47 'The Menace of Grey Squirrels', *The Field*, 21 February 1931, p. 239.
48 Editorials, *The Field*, 23 May 1931, p. 731 ; 31 October 1931, p. 645, 'The Agreements at Ottawa,' *Country Life*, 27 August 1932, p. 227.
49 Letter from May Armstrong, *Country Life* , July 4 1931 p. 24.
50 Letter from Robert Wills ,*The Field*,18 April 1931; article by R. I. Pocock ' Will Grey Squirrels mate with Red?', *The Field*, 2 May 1931, p. 623.
51 Editorial, *The Field*, 7 November 1931.
52 *Hansard* vol 246, 8 December 1930, p. 49–51; vol 249, 2 March 1931,. p. 19–20; vol 251, 20 April 1931, p. 598–9; vol 252, 21 May 1931 p. 2192–3
53 *Hansard* vol 252, 14 May 1931, p. 1367–8.
54 Editorial *The Field*,10 January 1931, p. 35; 'Menace of Grey Squirrels,' 21 February 1931, p. 239 .
55 'Menace of Grey Squirrels', *The Field*, 21 February 1931, p. 239; 16 May 1931, p. 693.
56 Cheviot, 'The Menace of Grey Squirrels', *The Field*, 23 May 1931, p. 740.
57 Cheviot , 'The Menace of Grey Squirrels', *The Field*, 23 May 1931, p. 740; letter from Richard Hale ,*The Field*, 21 November 1931, p. 781.
58 'The Grey Squirrel,' *Country Life*, 23 May 1931, p. xlviii.
59 *The Grey Squirrel*, Ministry of Agriculture Advisory Leaflet no 58 1931.
60 *The Grey Squirrel*, Ministry of Agriculture Advisory Leaflet no 58 1931.
61 Destructive Imported Animals Act 1932, which became law in March 1932. *Hailsbury's Statutes* vol 2 1991. For responses to the muskrat and rats which move like 'Attila's hordes' see A D Middleton ,'Muskrats in Great Britain. A New Danger to the Country', *The Field*, 29 August 1931, p. 319; Viscount Lymington ' The Vermin Toll on Farming', *The Field*, 5 September 1931, p. 353.
62 See E.S. Turner, *All Heaven in a Rage* , Centaur, West Sussex, 1992, pp. 310–312; Ministry of Agriculture and Fisheries Advisory Committee on Myxomatosis, *Myxomatosis.Second Report of the Advisory Committee on Myxomatosis* (HMSO, London 1955); Kean, *Animal Rights*, p. 199.
63 *The Grey Squirrel*, Ministry of Agriculture and Fisheries Leaflet no 58, Revised Edition 1954.
64 H. G. Lloyd, 'Past and Present Distribution of Red and Grey Squirrels', *Mammal Review*,vol 13 no 2/3/4 1983, p 75.
65 Raphael Samuel, *Theatres of Memory*, Verso, London, 1994, p. 139.
66 'Back to Nature,' Highland Wildlife Park, Kincraig, Kingussie, Inverness-shire, Scotland, 1999
67 In similar vein to the 'beast of Dartmoor': is this an escaped leopard or large cat seen by imaginative drunks?
68 Sally J. Morgan, 'The ghost in the luggage. Wallace and Braveheart: post-colonial 'pioneer' identities,' *European Journal of Cultural Studies* vol 2(3) 1999.
69 Thousands of tons of sand and gravel disappeared after three days of storms in Autumn 1999. 'Disappearing village. Sea claims another piece of Dunwich', *The Guardian*, 22 October 1999.
70 Caption on natural landscape cabinet at Dunwich Museum, Suffolk, May 1999.
71 V. P. W. Lowe and A. S. Gardiner, ' Is the British Squirrel (Sciurus Vulgaris Leucourus Kerr) British?', *Mammal Review*, vol 13: 2/3/4/ June /Sept/ Dec 1983 pp. 57–67.
72 See Angus Calder, *Myth of the Blitz*, Jonathan Cape, London, 1991.

Avebury and other not-so-ancient places: the making of the English heritage landscape

Brian Edwards

Of all the hundreds of wonderful places in the region my favourite is Avebury, a huge stone circle near Marlborough, it makes Stonehenge look like something the scouts put up.

John Fortune, *English Country Cottages*, 1998.

The earthwork at Avebury is perhaps the most impressive prehistoric monument in Wiltshire, and in scale and conception ranks among the foremost works of prehistoric man in Europe. The site is less widely known than Stonehenge, and the visitor approaches it with fewer preconceived ideas of its appearance.

Nikolaus Pevsner, *The Buildings of England: Wiltshire*, 1963.

A tour of 'Prehistoric Avebury'

The village of Avebury is situated in Wiltshire's Kennet valley some 10 km west of Marlborough, and approximately 30 km north of Stonehenge. In Avebury's midst the chalk downlands are home to the largest concentration of prehistoric monuments in Europe, a spectacular number of sites of archaeological interest that includes the remains of the sarsen cap from which it is assumed the stones at Stonehenge were mined. Highly featured in guidebooks and archaeological tomes, the 'Avebury Complex', as the World Heritage Site at Avebury has become known in heritage speak, incorporates six 'key historic monuments' in the 'care of the state'.

Managed by the National Trust in partnership with English

Heritage, the six designated sites are said to originate from the Neolithic period and to have been in use around 3000 BC – some 1,500 years before Stonehenge was built. The six sites include Windmill Hill – Europe's largest causewayed enclosure remotely located some 2 km north west of Avebury; Silbury Hill – Europe's largest 'man-made mound' 1.5 km to the south'; West Kennett Long Barrow – the largest chambered tomb in England, on a footpath 2 km south; and the Sanctuary – the former site of a concentric stone and wooden circle 2 km to the south east.

Avebury itself is home to the Great Stone Circle – the remains of the largest stone circle in Europe surrounded by a ditch and bank enclosing an area of twenty-eight acres that also features some smaller stone groupings; and West Kennett Avenue – the remains of a parallel line of similar sarsen stone megaliths that although incomplete stretches away from Avebury towards the Sanctuary. Some of the boulders at Avebury are as large as any of those at Stonehenge, but not having been fashioned appear in a more natural state.

The making of the English heritage landscape
Although the 'Great Stone Circle' at Avebury in Wiltshire is rather less well known than that icon of 'Prehistoric Britain' Stonehenge, many of those familiar with the 'Avebury Complex' are aware that it is far older than its more famous neighbour. The reaction therefore might be surprise were it suggested that the 'prehistory' that visitors to Avebury come to see is a product of the twentieth century.

Although few visitors are aware of it, the English heritage landscape at Avebury is an amalgam of differing ideas. It is not as prehistory left it, nor is it as the local population would have it. It is more something manufactured in the near past by the heritage industry than fashioned in the far past by our ancestors. This modern remaking of the landscape started with Avebury's rediscovery by a seventeenth-century antiquarian, and from that point the 'prehistoric' landscape started diverging from the organic landscape. It has been continually remade ever since, but no more so than in the twentieth century, when most of what we see today was constructed. Avebury is valued for its prehistory, yet what people have come to recognise as prehistoric Avebury – the vast number of stones in the circle and the avenue – was erected in the

1930s by marmalade heir Alexander Keiller.

Avebury is now labelled a monument, but it was not a monument until Alexander Keiller wrote himself into its history in the 1920s through his interest as an amateur archaeologist. Until he unearthed stones buried by farmers and superstitious Christians and cast them upright in cement Avebury was a village with a living and thriving community. It had all the accoutrements of the imagined quintessential English village, with a large number of people living their lives around their church, chapels, hall, social club, sports clubs, shops, guest houses, hotel, pub, farms, garages, butchers, bakers, and even saddlemakers. The parish of Avebury had a monument within its vicinity; it was not a monument with a village located within it.[1]

An unluckily placed village

It was the eighteenth century antiquarian William Stukeley, due to his early mapping and drawing at Avebury looked upon as the founder of field archaeology in England, who proclaimed that the complex had 'fallen sacrifice to the wretched ignorance and avarice of a little village unluckily plac'd within it'.[2] The notion that this was a landscape endangered by the local community had been fed by John Aubrey, who having rediscovered the complex in the previous century is widely acknowledged as the father of archaeology in England. And Avebury in danger is an idea that has been added to ever since by a succession of eminent conservationists. But what they continually overlooked is how the interaction of the community with the Avebury landscape is crucial to our understanding of this place.

Whereas Stonehenge is a prehistoric outpost secluded from ongoing life, Avebury is an occupied place, a landscape continually inhabited since before written culture, before royalty, and before state interference. Human cohabitation with the stones is what has made it unique and fascinating. It is common for Stonehenge tourists to express disappointment with the 'visitor experience', and this dissatisfaction has usually been connected with the crowds of other visitors and the roar of traffic. Such disappointments are rarely expressed at Avebury, because visitors are aware of the village and therefore expect other people to be there.[3]

The making of 'Prehistoric Avebury'

Sharing the Avebury complex with the community was not on the agenda of Alexander Keiller, after he involved himself with the Avebury landscape through his purchase of Windmill Hill in 1923.[4] His interest as an amateur archaeologist had brought him to the area, and his fantastic wealth allowed him to dabble in the landscape in a fashion that would not otherwise have been possible. Even then there probably would not have been any further interest had his excavations not brought such instantaneous results. Windmill Hill revealed itself to be a Neolithic settlement however, at the time of discovery unique in being the largest complex of its kind in Europe.[5] Encouraged by his find Keiller purchased the Manor House and as much of the monument, houses and surrounding land, that he could obtain. He then gathered his friends about him and set about changing the course of landscape history.

Guided by handmade copies of antiquarian surveys and the Reverend A.C.Smith's guide to the location of eighteen large sarsen stones 'sunk deep in the ground',[6] Keiller disrupted the landscape of half a millennium. Where he discovered stones that were buried in the vicinity of the henge and the Avenue, he placed them upright in reinforced concrete. He erected stones not visible when Stukeley surveyed Avebury in the early years of the eighteenth century, and fashioned a landscape that no one in Avebury's history would have recognised by placing concrete markers where a receptor pit was evident but no stone was found.[7] He even placed a marker where he thought a megalith should have been, but in fact no stone nor pit was discovered.[8]

During the period when the rest of Britain was preparing to 'Dig For Britain' and plant food, Keiller planted boulders in sequestered allotments that had been in constant use since they were introduced to ward off the pauperism that had led to the Swing Riots in 1830.[9] Instead of feeding the nation, the common pound was converted into a megalith garden. It was here Keiller planted a stone found in the fabric of a house, which had lost several chunks to the stone cutters who were building roads and houses, and had come to resemble a Henry Moore sculpture. As this stone had lost any identifying shape that could be compared with Stukeley's drawings, Keiller had no evidence that the location he chose for it was the actual position it occupied at any time during prehistory.

Like so many stones he replaced, it could not for certain be ascertained which way it faced, nor which way up it was originally; but he concreted it in place nonetheless. First harvested in prehistory and placed no one knows how or where, knocked over perhaps by a jealous Church, buried for the convenience of farmers, harvested again by eighteenth-century builders, and once again by a twentieth-century renovator who despite the missing components bolted what he could back together and put it on display, this stone says much about the English heritage landscape. That it came from an Aveburian's home demolished to provide a High Street view of the circle makes an ironic coda.

Avebury demolished
Fronting a conservation movement backed by the Ministry of Works and the Rural District Council, Keiller started a tradition of demolishing houses and other buildings within the Avebury circle.[10] When he gave Avebury to 'the nation', the National Trust continued demolishing properties in its care. Conservation arguments against the aesthetic and archaeological damage that might be incurred by the introduction of modern provision for dealing with water, sewage and electricity ensured further destruction. Photographs taken by local people provide evidence of the destruction, but they do not wholly convey the effect on either the community, the history of Avebury, or the landscape.[11] That this policy was carried out by 'conservation bodies' with ruthless efficiency and with complete disregard to the history of the place, particularly for the Saxon, late medieval, and enclosure history of the landscape, says much about how single-minded the heritage industry had become. Such a high profile figure within the National Trust as James Lees-Milne, did not 'approve of the proposal to destroy the old village within the circle', or the plan to 'remove medieval cottages and clear away all traces of habitation subsequent to the Iron Age'.[12] Yet his thoughts were confined to his diary. Thus a National Trust, supposedly with obligations under the terms of Keiller's will, continued to destroy evidence of continuity of occupation within the site, and with it evidence of the integration between the landscape and the community.

Through its accumulative scars from prehistoric earthworks to historic tofts and buildings, the interwoven eclectic nature

Swindon Road Cottages before and during demolition

of Avebury's heritage was indicative of its past, and the very thing conservationists should be expected to preserve. Yet preservationists followed the traditions of builders, farmers, and early and medieval Christians who wrought havoc in order to adapt the landscape to their own narrow vision. That this single-minded destruction took place despite the introduction of increasingly potent legislation to protect historic sites is quite incredible. The Ancient Monuments Protection Act 1900 was introduced to protect medieval remains and required permission to be sought to demolish such property. The National Trust Act 1907 was supposed to ensure that property left to or acquired by the Trust could not be radically altered. The Ancient Monuments Act 1931 required local authorities to protect not only monuments but the areas surrounding them.[13] All of this legislation was imposed during the four decades prior to the campaign of destruction. Yet it was the National Trust, the Ministry of Works, and the local authority, with these protective powers, who worked to remove the inconvenient parts that did not conform in order to present a uniform vision of the heritage of the site.

Avebury relocated
A general local housing shortage was exacerbated by the destruction of property in Avebury, as the many homes that were demolished had not outlived their usefulness. If the aesthetics and historical value they contained did not ensure their survival, then being required as homes and housing stock for a community base also failed to justify their existence. It is perhaps obvious that local people would be particularly upset by the destruction of their village and the breakup of their community, especially as some of the evictions were particularly harrowing. The unpleasant upheavals, combined with the still very real threat of the workhouse and the living memory of the evil visited upon victims of tied evictions in neighbouring Compton Bassett and Cherhill, created a threatening unease.[14] The Rural District Council was therefore obliged to appease villagers and solve this conservation imposed crisis in housing. Following the National Trust's acquisition of Avebury in 1942,[15] agreement was eventually reached that Trusloe, a hamlet a mile south-west of Avebury, should be the site for all local rehousing, and the decision to expand the housing at Trusloe was ratified by the Council in 1946.[16]

The decision to build at Trusloe has proved particularly ironic, as archaeological research during 1999 has demonstrated that William Stukeley's much maligned suggestion of a second avenue to Beckhampton was indeed accurate. His drawings of the 1720s highlighted a second avenue of parallel stones similar to the West Kennet Avenue, leaving Avebury's west opening and curving round south west towards

Beckhampton. As John Aubrey had not catalogued these stones some sixty years before Stukeley, however, it was frequently proclaimed that Stukeley had invented this avenue to fit what were considered his rather fantastic theories.[17] Thus discredited despite his accurate recordings, Stukeley's 'Beckhampton Avenue' was consigned to myth and housing eventually erected in its path. The new housing sits directly between the circle and a newly found prehistoric enclosure, with Trusloe as it stands today cutting through the line of a now invisible prehistoric 'Beckhampton Avenue'.[18]

The displacement and relocation of the community to Trusloe has not only resulted in encroachment on prehistoric 'brown' sites, however. It has also meant the dislocation of the people from the central places of church, chapel, club, school, pub, shop and garage. To get to these essential facilities villagers now face a hazardous walk along the busy and pavementless A4361, or a traipse across a muddy footpathed field that the parish council has lobbied to have metalled for half a century. Without this path the few remaining indigenous Aveburians remain remote from their locale, and without the people who gave the village substance the everyday life has been taken out of Avebury, and the landscape has become a dead artefact. Whatever the Avebury complex was intended for it was always a living landscape, but its heart has been taken out. The tourists that replace the indigenous people on the streets weave confusion where once there were the reassuring rhythms of a living community. Visitors now traipse through what is left of the village as they visit the monument, blissfully unaware that their surroundings were once very different indeed.

Properties that remain in Avebury house relatively few of the indigenous population, and none of those who were forced to move to the hamlet of Trusloe would be able to afford to return to Avebury village as the property prices in this heritage haven have spiralled even beyond other places in Wiltshire. Even if former inhabitants could afford a comparable property they would not be able to return to Avebury, as due to the eradication programme only upmarket buildings remain. There is now a noticeable absence of the formerly large number of small cottages that characterised the centre of the village for more than three centuries.[19] Surviving photographs and memories tell a sorry tale of cottages demolished, houses knocked down, trees eradicated, gardens and allotments laid bare, workshops liquidated, chapels making way for car parks, historic homes converted into custodian flats, stables into public toilets, village stores and farm buildings into gift shops. The history of these places has been eradicated and families and a community displaced.[20] It seems unbelievable after the centenary of the National Trust that it was this conservation body that was in charge of the destruction meted out in the thirty years after it took over the guardianship of Avebury in 1942, but what is most surprising is that the architectural cleansing of Avebury appears to be continuing.[21]

The continuance of the English heritage landscape

Since 1976, the National Trust has frequently declared that it no longer seeks to demolish buildings within Avebury.[22] Despite this reassurance, however, the conversion of Avebury into a heritage related commodity continues in subtle ways. The former stable block that appears on the cover of the District Council's publication *Avebury; Archaeology of the District* is also a central feature on a post card, jigsaw, and box of fudge on sale in the National Trust shop and Alexander Keiller Museum. Yet this stable no longer exists. Having been a feature of the Avebury landscape when commercial products bearing the stable were introduced in the early 1990s, the photograph illustrating the cover of the 1998 issue of the Ordnance Survey Explorer 157 covering Avebury reveals that the stable is no more. The roof has been demolished and only the outer walls of the stable remain, and they are retained only because they form part of a garden boundary. The disappearance of the former stable was completed at the behest of the National Trust, and illustrates an ongoing agenda. There are examples of similar walls nearby, none of which are capped to prevent the rain from causing their eventual collapse. Within yards of the former stable site a building's ancient timber frame is exposed to the elements that will inevitably cause its downfall, as cladding has been attached to the inside rather than over the frame to protect it. This subtle erosion proceeds unnoticed, and follows attempts by the Trust within recent memory to quietly 'sound out' the reaction of Avebury Parish Council to Trust plans to demolish the only remaining cottages on the main road through Avebury.[23]

The cottages the National Trust wanted to demolish were

at one time Pratt's the saddlers and the general stores. They were not only some of the few remaining small buildings in the village, but some of the few survivors of Avebury's service industry once serving the main London–Bath/Bristol coach route. The saddlers and the other village trades of blacksmiths, wheelwrights, ropemakers, and coopers, were championed at the Museum of Wiltshire Rural Life in Avebury's seventeenth-century Great Barn. Here Victorian Avebury was recreated using the tools of now defunct trades and industries, and these were exhibited alongside superseded agricultural equipment. This museum has also disappeared, however, despite successfully attracting a high percentage of visitors and generating substantial income.

During the mid-1990s the National Trust laid plans to open a new high-tech museum in the Great Barn, and made Lottery and Millennium Fund applications prior to announcing its intentions to the leaseholder the Wiltshire Rural Life Society. Despite the failure of its application on grounds that were highly critical of the Trust's plans, the Wiltshire Rural Life Society reluctantly agreed to surrender its extensive lease and this ultimately resulted in the loss to Avebury of more fragments of its history. The list included the tools of the local sarsen cutting industry, the accoutrements of Pratt's the saddlers, the blacksmith's equipment from the last working forge, the ropemaker's winch, the largest single collection of historic photographs of Avebury, and an irreplaceable Avebury archive. This historic collection is now in storage at Lackham College, because the National Trust deemed that it was 'not Avebury relevant'.[24]

Avebury Great Barn
At the Millennium the National Trust is now the sole purveyor of official history in Avebury, and is planning an expansion of the Alexander Keiller Museum in the Great Barn, which they plan to rename. Ironically, the Trust had attempted to demolish this magnificent building in the 1960s, and it was only the intervention of a protest group including conservation guru John Betjeman that halted the barn's imminent disappearance. Eventually, the Wiltshire Rural Life Society originated a proposal to finance the reconstruction of the barn, and the National Trust was forced to concede that the Great Barn could remain part of the landscape.[25] At the time it was saved,

a series of early nineteenth-century farm buildings were clustered around the main barn in the north section of the yard which formed the Avebury Manor Farmyard. All these buildings would soon be demolished, however, in the name of conservation.[26] It was thought that the money to renovate the whole yard could not be raised, and the size of the overall project may have endangered the restoration of the Great Barn. The other buildings were therefore sacrificed, and disappeared from the landscape. Ironically, these buildings would have provided much needed museum space in Avebury at the Millennium, but like the adjacent Manor it was something the National Trust was not interested in at the time.

The Avebury experience
Avebury Manor had received fee-paying visitors since 1955, as 'The Home of Sir Francis and Lady Knowles'.[27] The tradition was continued by others including the Marquess of Ailesbury, and no objection was raised against the 'thousands of visitors' or the introduction of ticket kiosks and 'seasonal mobile refreshment shops'. Modified driveways, temporary car parks, and the grills and fencing to facilitate a zoo were installed during this period of heritage enterprise seemingly without comment; but this was not the case when a St Albans builder bought Avebury Manor and planned to open an 'Elizabethan Experience' on Good Friday 1989.[28] The indigenous population welcomed the employment opportunities introduced by Ken King's Elizabethan Experience, and enjoyed the chance to enter the Manor for free for the first time. The National Trust had other ideas, however, and combined in opposition with Kennet District Council and 'Avebury in Danger', a pressure group headed by lofty incomers. The Manor opened with Elizabethan players, falconry, and Civil War displays, and closed under a deluge of planning refusals. The Elizabethan Experience was, in short, bankrupted.[29] A scheme for a hotel opposite the Sanctuary on nearby Overton Hill met a similar fate,[30] as did a renovation scheme proposed at West Kennett Farm.[31] To prevent any further innovations the National Trust purchased each of these sites, demolishing anything that didn't suit prior to invoking its plan to impose its own National Trust experience on Avebury.

The National Trust experience is imposed upon Avebury with the ever approving nod of English Heritage, which is looking to step down from responsibilities at Avebury once its millennium Management Plan is implemented.[32] This will leave the National Trust in sole control of the official philosophy of Avebury's heritage.[33] First, however, English Heritage intends to further redesign the map of the World Heritage Site with its river, hedges and parish boundaries. This is not being carried out in order to recreate a prehistoric landscape, but in order to make the monument more significant.[34] What this means is that the countryside surrounding the monument will not be cultivated by farmers in the manner it would be if the monuments were absent, nor will the agriculture revert to being landscaped as it was during prehistory, or managed as it was at any other time in history. The environs of the monument are to be managed as a setting, a Hollywood style backdrop to the World Heritage Site. English Heritage evidently expects to continue Keiller's example by placing its own interpretation on the landscape, and altering the setting to match this vision.

Avebury and other not-so-ancient places of the English heritage landscape

And what of that not-so-ancient place Stonehenge? It has not escaped the attentions of the heritage industry: a stone was straightened and set in concrete in 1901, six further stones in 1919 and 1920, three more in 1959, and four in 1964. There was also the excavation of the Altar stone and re-erection of the Triathlon in 1958. Now English Heritage has a 'master plan' to build a tunnel to put the landscape back to 'how it was'!

Instead of the cathedral that Aubrey boasted that we had inherited, no matter how reduced by the ravages of time, our ancient past is a ruination plundered by early antiquarians and despoiled by the heritage industry appropriating control of these sites from Avebury's community. Our legacy is the result of an amateur fad for restoration that has seen the twentieth century redesigning a 5,000 year old landscape that had no importance attached to it for more than two millennia.[35] Yet the heritage industry has latched on to the fascination early antiquarians had for prehistory with complete disregard for a closer past and the equally important issues that surround it. Such has been the impact on the landscape that the monuments at Avebury and Stonehenge which future generations will inherit are neither the creation of prehistoric peoples nor of the communities who have occupied these lands during history. The future will instead inherit something constructed by the heritage industry. The instigators of the English heritage landscape were essentially amateurs, working by trial and error. They operated independently of any recognised method, or governed practice, or any local or national consensus of approval. Yet their landscape is endorsed and promoted as our collective cultural heritage by the custodians of our past who omit the extent of modern interference and reconstruction from their guides and museum displays.

When a site such as Avebury is adopted by the heritage industry, a single body effectively takes control of the view of history available to the visitor and the site goes through a process of sanitising which reduces it to one facet.[36] Such singular views of the past promotes false ideas that wholly distort historical perspectives, and in doing so send powerful messages that overwhelm any tendencies for alternative lines of enquiry. The English heritage landscape plies us with false images, creating a presence for itself in the national consciousness that affects our feelings about the past. Its message is saturated with suggested greatness, that in turn promotes belief in a time when we were part of a nation with one voice. We have to look beyond this, however, as the heritage industry is persistent in its efforts to remake England and to preserve a perceived unity through archetypal images and patriotic histories.[37] We must scrape away at the surface of our treasured sites as a modern-day archaeologist would search around a precious find, to reveal not only the layers of time, but expose the fragmented society which created and maintained the English heritage landscape.

Notes
1. Michael Dames, *The Avebury Cycle*, Thames and Hudson, London, 1976, p. 9.
2. William Stukeley, *Abury*, W. Innys, London, 1743, p. 16.
3. National Trust and Bournemouth University Avebury visitor surveys 1998, Alexander Keiller Museum, Avebury.
4. Keiller was encouraged to buy Windmill Hill to prevent Marconi from establishing a radio tower on the site.
5. I.F.Smith, 'Excavations at Windmill Hill, Avebury, Wilts', in *Wiltshire Archaeological Magazine* 57, 1959–60, pp. 149-62.
6. A.C.Smith, *Guide to the British and Roman Antiquities of the North Wiltshire Downs*, Marlborough College Natural History Society, Devizes, 1885, see especially pp. 139–40.
7. Holding a megalith upright requires a form of footing to support the sarsen

stone, and it was on these empty receptor pits that Keiller placed concrete markers.
8 See Michael Pitts, *Footprints Through Avebury*, Avebury, Stones Restaurant, 1985.
9 Brian Edwards, 'Village Labour : Allotments and Arson', and 'Transportation and Emigration', both in Wiltshire Life Society, *Wiltshire Folklife* 30, Spring 1995, pp. 20–36.
10 The Avebury Preservation Scheme launched in 1937.
11 See the photographic collection of the Wiltshire Rural Life Society, held at the time of writing at the National Trust, Alexander Keiller Museum, Avebury.
12 James Lees Milne, *Diaries: Ancestral Voices*, John Murray, London, 1995, see 2 April, 1942.
13 See Jane Fawcett (ed), *The Future of the Past : Attitudes to conservation 1174–1974*, Thames & Hudson, London, 1976.
14 See Arthur Cleverley in, Wiltshire Family History Society, *Wiltshire Family History*, January 1995, pp. 28–33; Brian Edwards, 'Hodge – a tale worth retelling' in, Wiltshire Life Society, *Wiltshire Folklife* 34, Spring 1997, pp. 19–26.
15 See 'Avebury acquisition of the National Trust', *The Times*, 23 March 1943.
16 In Avebury Parish Minutes (c/o the Parish Clerk) there are three spellings : Trulsoe, Truslow, and Truslowe.
17 That the completed Avebury must have resembled a snake, with the Sanctuary as its head, the West Kennet Avenue being the body with the Stone Circle its main coil, and the second parallel line of stones as its tail.
18 Leicester University, University of Wales (Newport), Southampton University: combined dig August–September 1999.
19 E. Storey, *Report of County Planning Officer 1948–1955*, Wiltshire County Council, Trowbridge, 1955; E. Storey, *County Development Plan Written Statements*, Wiltshire County Council, Trowbridge, 1947; E. Storey, 'County Map (Avebury Inset Map) Proposal' in *County Development Plan Written Statements and the County and Town Map Area* , Wiltshire County Council, Trowbridge, February 1953; E.Storey, *Report and Analysis of the Development Plan for Wiltshire 1952*, Wiltshire County Council, Trowbridge, 1947. See also opinion of 1979 pattern of settlement in *Victoria County History*, vol XII, 1983, p. 90.
20 The photograph collection of the Wiltshire Rural Life Society, held at the time of writing by the National Trust, Alexander Keiller Museum, Avebury.
21 Patrick Wright, *A Journey Through Ruins*, Flamingo, London, 1992, Part One and Part Two, especially pp. 62, 67–73, 78–97, 157–66.
22 National Trust Wessex Regional Office mission statements presented to Wiltshire Rural Life Society 1976-1997. See archive of the Wiltshire Rural Life Society, Lackham College, Lacock, Wilts.
23 Oral testimony of the Parish Clerk and the village Postmaster.
24 National Trust, letter to the Curator Great Barn, 11 October 1995. See correspondence files of Wiltshire Rural Life Society, Lackham College, Lacock, Wilts.
25 Established in 1975 to develop fresh enthusiasm and public interest in the social, domestic, and economic history of Wiltshire. Wiltshire Rural Life Society, *Project Brief*, 19.9.80.
26 Detail from *Wiltshire Archaeological Magazine*, XIX, p. 21.
27 *Avebury Manor : The Home of Sir Francis and Lady Knowles*, English Life Publications, Avebury, 1962.

28 'Old Manor brings past back to life', *Wiltshire Gazette & Herald*, 16 March 1989.
29 Michael Pitts, 'What Future for Avebury ?', unpublished essay c/o Stones Restaurant Avebury, 1990.
30 See Kennet District Council Planning Department reference: West Overton/Ashley K 3088/89. See also Wiltshire Archaeological and Natural History Society Library, Devizes Museum Cuttings reference : 31.52, 31.53, 31.56, 31.57, 31.65, 31.80, 31.81, 31.87, 31.88, 31.93, 31.100, 31.101, 31.106, 31.123, 31.126, 31.145, 31.146, 31.148, 31.151, 31.152.
31 Kennet District Council Planning Ref: West Kennet/Marlborough Homes. See also Wiltshire Archaeological and Natural History Society Library, Devizes Museum Cuttings Ref: 31.360
32 The draft proposal was finally announced in the national press 17 April 1998. See especially *Western Daily Press*, pp. 24–29.
33 English Heritage, *Conservation Bulletin*, March 1995, pp. 3–4.
34 Melanie Pomeroy, *Avebury World Heritage Site Management Plan*, English Heritage, London, 1998.
35 Peter Fowler makes this point in terms of 'reverence for the stones' in 'Avebury', *History Today*, January 1995, p. 12.
36 See David Lowenthal, *The Heritage Crusade and the Spoils of History*, 1997, Cambridge University Press, Cambridge, pp. 156–162.
37 Raphael Samuel 'Introduction : exciting to be English' in, Raphael Samuel (ed), *Patriotism: The Making and Unmaking of British National Identity*, Routledge, London, Vol. I, 1989.

Putting gender into seafaring: representing women in public maritime history

Jo Stanley

I write this as the female child of Liverpool seafarers: the port-based great-grandchild of a ship's barber who brought embroidered kimonos from Japan, in which I later dressed. He was a man who put the excitement and the biography in 'sea' for me. I write as the daughter of a Royal Naval wireless operator who fed me story morsels about crowded ships echoing with masculinity and let me play with banknotes from Madagascan quaysides. These enabled me to envisage the 'away at sea life', a world in which I did not figure, There was no space for 'little girl sailor' in 'Navy' or even 'abroad'. Yet now I write as feminist traveller.

I write above all as the great-niece of a stewardess for Merseyside's Elder Dempster line, May Quinn, who sailed to West Africa but left no stories, no snaps, just millions of foreign beads and exotic souvenirs. The silence was an inadvertent legacy so profound that it challenged me in the 1970s as feminist historian, to find the answers to a foundational question: *were* women at sea then? That is, could this foreign territory belong to me and my sex? Did we have a public, and even challenging, place beyond the private domestic milieu? I later researched further questions. How were women at sea? Why were they at sea? What did they do? Why? What were their relations with seamen (such as Dad)? What difference did they make on ships? And above all, why don't we know about women's connections with the seas. Why isn't it written about or on public display?

I write as a feminist and knowledge worker now profound-

Masculine superstitions about women's presence on ship offer scope for researchers into gender relations at sea: *Murphy's Law,* **by Jim Storey**

ly involved in the worldwide promotion and publicising of women's maritime studies. My desire is to create a more gender-balanced, gender-aware maritime history, where the ways I and other women view sea-life are fully represented; and where gender differences are an exciting area for exploration. This is not exclusively for women's ends and has the generous goal of creating public presentations of our maritime past which show the full complexity of women *and* men in maritime history. We need to not just to restore that absent 'wo' in sea..men and not just expand 'maritime' to include port communities. We need to explore the gender relations, illustrated, for example, in Captain Sally Fodie's autobiography[1] (see illustrations: Respect Earned and Murphy's Law). How have polarities been produced, what do they say about society and how do they affect the women subjected to them, and the men who are so extraordinarily emotional about claiming the ship as exclusively male site?

Public histories must discuss the meanings and long -term social effects of women's absence from representation and from the literal and metaphorical seas. They must explore the reasons why women (and thereby men) are portrayed in these ways. Epistemologically, it means exploring why and how women – 'the devil's ballast'[2] – have been so written out of public history. What are the effects of such erasure from public record? Leading cultural theorist Pierre Bourdieu has argued in relation to working-class museum visitors that practice (for example explanatory panels) must proclaim 'the right not to know, the right to be there in ignorance, the right of the ignorant to be there'.[3] I believe that similarly maritime museums must proclaim to women visitors the right to find themselves there; the right to be there – ignorantly or wisely; the right to know that they have always been connected with the sea; the right to know why they are not represented there; the right to know why there is such ignorance about their presence; and the right to know the differences that their presences and absences make both in lived history and in historiography. This more balanced historical account can be created by displaying gender-aware exhibits and encouraging debate and a historiography that discusses the complex social, economic and psychoanalytic ideas behind the exclusions and myths.

Maritime museums and their absent artefacts

A museum might be defined as an essentially object-based informational service in a permanent location, run for public benefit not profit,[4] and therefore with a responsibility to offer accurate (and even empowering?) data and pleasurable range of learning experiences. But, as Southampton museum workers Sian Jones and Sharon Pay argue, in our society 'the exclusion of women's experience is most evident in the public arena of the museum.'[5] Museums in general have, until recently, been one of the last remaining areas of historiographical silence about women's presence. Therefore this responsibility is not being adequately met. Silences and absences specifically about women and the sea have been perhaps most apparent not in maritime books but in public history: the ex-Empire's maritime museums and heritage sites in the UK and overseas. The three basic problems were, and to some extent still are: firstly, a focus on shipping as a formal public activity related to national power and warfare and exceptional to normal life; secondly, an absence of exhibits about people; and thirdly, the notion that sea is nothing to do with the land and the domestic.

Naval warfare

Many maritime museums have extensive exhibits on naval warfare and distant patriarchal figures of technical and political prowess such as Admiral Nelson. In this way the museums position woman as not only insignificant to maritime history – which matters when national pride comes from that maritime past – but also construct a history of woman as inactive in, even ineligible for, participation in the maritime workforce of seafaring nations. According to Australian National Maritime Museum worker Mary-Louise Williams, at a conference one of her colleagues 'argued that "maritime history, or military history, simply are not sympathetic bases for women's history and no amount of creativity can achieve more than a minority presence." I think our critic is partly right ... male hegemony is extremely strong in maritime and military museums. This is not so much a criticism as a fact.'[6] If displays feature life *at* sea (which has been overwhelmingly male) and *official* history then women will necessarily be absent.

Ships not souls

Existing museum collections present a problem, an overabundance of evidence about vessels compared to the meagre number of exhibits about people. Museums generally have suffered from an over-focusing on objects rather than on the ordinary women and men who used them, and compounded that by giving domestic objects (e.g. irons) less priority than public objects such as guns. Maritime museums have essentially meant galleries full of showcase-bound model ships. Created with rational principles and scientific knowledge, these objects function as testimony that masculine abilities in making such products can overcome that chaotic, natural female force: the sea. But there has been little evidence affirming how working people actually made, and sailed, those endless ships displayed in seascapes and mathematically accurate miniatures. Borrowing the 1988 Victoria & Albert Museum advertising slogan 'an ace caff with a quite a nice museum attached', we might say that many maritime museums have meant, at worst, 'a lot of ships with a few posh Admirals attached.'

Neglecting material about ordinary people – shipwrights and sailors, officers and dockers – inevitably means that half the population (women) are particularly absent. It would be

Seeing History: Public History in Britain Now

Traditional men can find it difficult to adjust to women seafarers: *Respect Earned* **by Jim Storey**

invalid to argue that women worked at sea in great numbers: they were under one per cent of the UK maritime seagoing workforce before the 1980s.[7] But census figures indicate over 4,000 women worked at sea in the peak year 1931, which therefore means it is reasonable to assume that at least 10,000 women may have been employed on the sea in the last 100 years. Hundreds of thousands more women have sea connections as seafaring captain's wives, port landladies, and families of seafarers as well as working in shipping line offices. The 1921 census showed there were a hundred females in shipping services for every 2027 men, for example.[8] The omission of women is further compounded by a sin of commission: the gendered binary image of those few maritime workers who do appear. As the title of the key work on this maritime gender divide, *Iron Men, Wooden Women*,[9] argues, women in maritime historiography have been cast as inanimate timber (figureheads ergo muses, but also stoic supporters ashore) while seamen are iron, strong and inflexible (but not rusted by brine!). And images repeatedly insist on sea*men* out there in that public space the sea, being manful, valiant (and maybe suffering hardship) in contrast to women ashore in private domestic spaces, representing nurturing, finer rather than brutal values, fixity, and unsuitability for/inability to deal with that dangerous force, the sea.

Museologist Gaby Porter charges that in museums generally the roles of women are usually represented, as 'relatively passive, shallow, undeveloped, muted and close; the roles of men are, in contrast, relatively active, deep, highly developed, fully pronounced and open.'[10] In maritime museums it has been even worse. Woman is rarely represented as a significant unit within maritime society. Too often the sea is depicted as masculine territory peopled by active important gentlemen who are later made into grand statues. The word seafarer is all too often taken to be the sign for 'man', even 'a proper man' or 'daring, stoic masculinity, performed out there'. Women wait: on the beach, on the quay, sometimes poetically. In the imagery of social class, officer-echelon woman is Lady Nelson. She is sweet/noble, stay-at-home and chastely devoted. In the imagery of working-class mariners, woman is Jill Tar: the other half of Jack. She waves him off at the quayside: her feet never wet, her legs never trousered, her home always private, dry and unsinkable, her duty to be fecund. So we are not told if, when Jack sails off, Jill turns inland to manage her Wharf Street chandlery, go pilfering on the docks or provide sexual services for the next Jack.[11]

A telling example of women's allotted place in public maritime historiography comes from museum's borderland with heritage: souvenir merchandise. In the Royal Naval Museum's mail order catalogue the only visible reference to women (apart from a bone china mug labelled 'I am a mug for a sailor') is a page entitled 'A Gift for the Ladies'. This offers five clusters of options, all focused on decoration of the body or home: personal adornment (brooches in the shape of Royal Naval Crowns); cosmetics (the Emma Hamilton range of English Lavender – shower gel, spray cologne etc); domestic decorations which also refer to women's traditional needle skills (Bone China Thimbles showing HMS Victory, Admiral Nelson, RN flags and RN crest); a chance to sew a decorative object (HMS Victory embroidery design in counted cross-stitch); and finally another item of home decoration, a Bone China Bell showing HMS Victory.[12] Historian Robert Hewison argued that we 'must criticise the heritage industry before we drown in honey and aspic.'[13] The danger in the world of maritime public history is not of drowning but of its opposite: being beached in a backwater with only Admiralty issue matronly bosoms, sewing needles, sodden lacey handkerchiefs and visions of ourselves as noble and patriotic supporters ashore rather than bona fide workers at sea.

Sea versus shore
The third basic problem in maritime museology and historiography is the tradition of a shore/land divide. Traditionally in that murky romanticised area of thinking 'our maritime past', the sea life is not allowed a relationship with land. The seafarer (mainly masculine in this context) is not seen as supported by and connected to the back-up services which, as feminist writer Cynthia Enloe points out when writing about the military, were often denied and are still seen as less significant than the front line (in this case, the sea).[14] Historiography generally has long offered us tales based on private-public splits, failing to recognise men's public roles are frequently sustained by women's private labour. There is a need for 'land' to be added to 'seafarer' just as public needs to be related to private. It is significant that as late as 1995 maritime historian Henry William Flayhart III found it necessary to point out that 'oceanic history does not end when a ship arrives.'[15] And although maritime historian David Williams says that now current maritime historiography 'embrac[es] all aspects of man's relationship with the sea',[16] that use of man's to mean people's, shows how much gender still needs addressing. The category 'land life' may include 'woman' and 'man' but the category 'sea life' is solely a masculine terrain in many visions.

Women's absence
My research about women's presence and absence in maritime museums has focused especially on two leading British maritime museums, at Greenwich and Liverpool.[17] Over the past eighteen years I have visited a number of maritime museums in the UK, US, Europe and Pacific Rim. New to maritime history and museology, I was researching seawomen as a labour historian and fiction writer interested in finding visual and physical contexts for biographical oral evidence I had collected from liner stewardesses. It never rains in a heritage museum, Robert Hewison contends.[18] Similarly, I had found in maritime art and movies that no woman could ever have walked up a gangway unless she was a beautiful passenger (in James Tissot's painting 'Ramsgate', 1876), or a sassy, swash-

buckling exception (in films such as Anne of the Indies). So I hoped that these leading maritime museums would offer more realistic occupational information as a way to ground my interview data. But they did not, especially in the early days, and I was shocked at the lack of women's presence and of any gender awareness.

Since the 1980s I have worked for three museums and been connected to several more. My knowledge of the business changed but so has museum practice and maritime historiography. Now maritime museums clearly demonstrate their concern to represent women and even gender issues. Indeed, the National Maritime Museum runs an international Women and the Sea Network to foster scholarship on the subject. Galleries at Greenwich and Liverpool have been created specifically with women in mind. And the Director of the Royal Naval Museum has announced, 'We in maritime museums must attend belatedly to the wholesale neglect of women's role in maritime history, which has for too long diminished the quality and value of our work.'[19] The National Maritime Museum at Greenwich attracted 480,000 visitors in 1998, 48 per cent of them women. (the national average is 52 per cent).[20] Ten years ago the principal ways women were represented in the galleries and the shop were: weeping Jill Tars on plates showing Jack Tar leaving port; Emma, Lady Hamilton displayed as a romantic relic of that English Naval hero, Nelson; [21] women as alluring foreign sights seen by seafaring men, for example a princess seen on Captain Cook's south sea island voyage. In every case they were defined by their romantic and non-challenging connection with seafaring men rather than in their own right. They were the second sex, there as figureheads rather than flesh and blood women.

During a quantitative survey I did in December 1998[22] I found that the older galleries at Greenwich were perpetuating outworn views of maritime history. There were fourteen artefacts in the four galleries open that day, plus a further twenty-odd small objects relating to Emma, Lady Hamilton. However, there were non-sexist modern displays in the modern galleries, especially in the children's area. These included yachtswoman Tracy Edwards, captain of the first all-women round-the-world Whitbread race. Also, the announcer for the shipping forecast was female. In psychoanalytic terms museum shops offer transitional objects, consumer goods which enable us to take a museum back home with us. According to Greenwich's 1998 survey, 53 per cent of the women visited the museum shop (as opposed to 38 per cent of men),[23] which suggests an ideal opportunity to offer customers items of relevance to them. However, in the shop there were only six items referring to women, if we include domestic goods such as tea-towels. The only object relevant to women's maritime history was a postcard of that non-seafarer Emma Hamilton as Ariadne – who ironically happens to be one of the few goddesses *not* associated with the sea. The imbalance in the galleries was partly rectified by a May 1999 expansion which included an increased focus on exhibit about passengers. The new fashion and global garden galleries in Neptune Court were designed to especially appeal to women and the NMM marketing officer has found they do so.[24] This assists in two of the three basic problems I asserted above; now people – indeed women – and shore life are included

Merseyside Maritime Museum attracted 290,522 visitors in 1998, fifty-two per cent of whom were women, that is four per cent higher than Greenwich. Ten years ago I could not find enough women represented there to able to categorise them. I brought away the memory of an etching of pretty stewardesses in pinnies scabbing in the 1926 general strike and a postcard of a migrating mother in a steerage diorama. If, ten years ago, I had been the proverbial alien from space, newly landed, I would have deduced from these two museums that women in maritime history were not seafarers and were all young, sexually active creatures. I would have imagined that their main role function in life was to be left at home by their seafaring male partners – but that this was somehow both romantically tragic and had no economic and social repercussions. If exceptionally women *were* on ships, it was as passengers, not workers, and in standard roles, for example as mum making the beds. Finally I would have wondered why the rare women seafarers were only there in domestic roles and why they betrayed their striking workmates.

During my quantitative study in Liverpool in December 1998 I noted forty-six items on women, that is, one item every 3.1 minutes, by comparison to a woman every 2.6 minutes at Greenwich. Although the numerical ratio was worse than the National Maritime Museum's, many items referring to women were actually more substantial in size and complexity. Again in the modern galleries where staff had the opportunities to make improvements, everywhere where a woman *could* be used she was. For example, the Customs and Excise gallery dealt with people (including women), who had active roles, and the shore/sea interface. Visiting the shop, the women's maritime history objects I was able to take away were a reproduction of a Pacific Line poster featuring a potential woman passenger for a Sunshine tour. If I had had the inclination I could have also have bought a Titanic poster featuring Kate Winslet (as passenger), a poster of a Cunard woman passenger en route to America and stewardess Violet Jessop's autobiography, if it hadn't been out of stock. That is, I could have acquired evidence that women were seafaring workers and passengers – that the shore and sea had a connection. As this chapter goes to press, the new Lifelines Gallery is opening at Merseyside Maritime Museum. It is designed to represent the people of the maritime community and it makes efforts to show women. For example, of the six life-size models of seafarers, one is female; this generously over-states women's actual numerical relation to men (usually 1:100).

Why are women and gender absent?
The reasons why women and gender are absent or inadequately represented in museums in general have been discussed in many feminist essays on gendered collecting policies, notably by museums worker and theorist Gaby Porter. The most fundamental explanation is that exhibitions reflect (and structure) the society they come from. Just as women's (especially domestic) lives have not been accorded the same value as men's, so *evidence* of those lives are similar undervalued, and simply not collected. Therefore women are generally under-represented and misrepresented in most museums, not only maritime ones. A number of possible additional material and psychoanalytic explanations for the absence of women and gender from many maritime museums can be offered. Primarily they cluster round the legacy of a particular period in museum history, with its own viewpoints on whether people should be represented at all in displays, and on gender.

Mary-Louise Williams from the Australian National Maritime Museum points out that 'maritime museums were fostered by men, who collected material that was of interest to them and their own histories. More than most, maritime museums attract men to work in them...Almost all maritime museum managers are men. Many of the areas of interest for collecting and display relate to industries and endeavours that have primarily involved men.'[25] This is not to imply malign individual intent to exclude women and gender but to state that we all see what matters to us and what we want to see. As museum theorist Susan Pearce argues, 'the extended self which collections represent is intended to extend beyond the grave.'[26] Collecting is a strategy to solidify identity through objects. As such, women and men with traditional male views in leading positions in maritime museums may have tended to collect and display what will enhance for posterity their preferred idea of sea life as hermetically masculine, ordered and fundamentally associated with national power and technical prowess. The problem could be solvable by training, and employing those capable of seeing other realities.

Such masculine collecting and display practices can be reinforced by the attitudes of women donors. That is, the collecting problem may be worsened by what is *not* offered. Most women have internalised notions of lack of self-worth, therefore they are unlikely to conserve objects from their own lives. As Jones and Pay point out: 'The collection of objects related to women's work is inhibited because that work is undervalued, even by women.'[27] Instead, women may act as personal archivists of sea*men's* history, for example keeping their husband's medals, but not their own diaries where they discuss the difficulties of managing without him. Secondly, classed notions of 'value' and a museum's daunting image may mean ordinary domestic objects are not offered to this public place where prestige seems to be on display. Thirdly, many women seafarers were single and had no descendants who might pass on objects to museums.

Excluding the Other can give museum workers an illusion of safety. Using psychoanalyst Jacques Lacan's concepts, Gaby Porter argues that 'Rationality is established through the exclusion of the feminine: the knower (subject/masculine) splits himself from the known (object/feminine) and establishes dominance over it/her.'[28] Therefore, to exclude evidence of the feminine from a museum is to establish (masculine) order and power, to state that rationality and not chaos rule. Maritime museums have been notoriously orderly places, staffed in most cases by men habituated to the order of the navy that they now interpret for often unruly visitors. From such a vantage point it can be hard to envisage more embracing views of the sea beyond the patriarchal naval ship.

I believe that there is a further psychoanalytic explanation for the absence of representations of women in maritime museums, and indeed maritime historiography: the tendency of human beings to be attracted to the thing we most fear. Hence we may go to sea because what we fear in the world most is the mythical power of he 'Deep' with its monsters, storms, cosmic rhythms and hidden depths. The fear of the sea is a correct one. But to own to the moments of appropriate weakness and abject terror it provokes can be to fail to present oneself as 'properly courageous'. A seamless story of fearless masculine heroism can be more easily developed if there are no representatives of the feminine around to witness the shameful fear. Some males, especially ex-Royal Naval men, in maritime museology and historiography, may need to believe that everything to do with the emotions (including wives and needs for support, including reassurance, rest and nurture) is/should be safely left behind, ashore. Such a separation enables them to maintain the illusion that fears do not exist. And if women cannot be entirely wished away then the next best thing has to be to represent the feminine in such derogatory ways that it ceases to have any significance: hence the particularly negative representations of women in maritime museums.

This ties in with the natural desire to avoid the problematic. The human void in maritime museum exhibits, especially as it affects women, can be partly explained by Gaynor Kavanagh's point about the great silences in museums in general. A lecturer in museum studies, she believes these silences are 'in part at least, born of a preference some have for an approach that eliminates anything problematic in order to minimise the difficulties and discomforts involved in questioning culture. Such avoidance is achieved by not looking further than the fabric of the object itself and by only addressing generalised secondary sources. In such a view all lives, regardless of age, gender, sexuality, ethnicity or locality, are little more than added complications. This approach calmly avoids acknowledging that the chaos, contradictions and qualities of our lives are played out through the use of objects, space, sound and oral tradition – the very things that are the evi-

Seeing History: Public History in Britain Now

Women preparing the fish for curing at Grimsby. The exhibition at the National Fishing Heritage Centre attests to the realities behind the public image of women in the deep-sea fishing community.

dence-bearing substance of museum collections.'[29] For maritime museums, trying to explain dependent relations with the shore and the existence of women at sea has clearly been so uncomfortable that it has been avoided.

The comfortable has a strong relationship with the seemly (which is intimately connected to the manly and to class). Women on or connected to ships have been seen as out of (domestic) place and unseemly, especially those in the waterfront sex industry. Pictures and data about them remain in cartoons and books, not on museum display. Inhibitions about discussing money may mean that old wage packets, or records from shipping offices where the seafarer sought the work to ensure family survival, do not get collected and displayed. Complex officer-level unease about alcohol abuse can mean an absence of captioned photos showing the dockland pubs where the seaman drank with/without his wife while on leave. Oral testimony about how women seafarers coped with menstruation and pregnancy might well be seen as too distastefully 'personal', even offensive, to exhibit. According to Kavanagh, 'museums have been overly conscious of public sensitivity – whose existence they often only assume – and cautious to the point of crippling self-censorship'.[30] Maritime museums especially may have suffered because they have been so dominated by Royal Naval officers accustomed to largely masculine institutions. Such a situation leads to tradition-bound men seeing many subjects (e.g. the details of childbirth) as women's matters that males should sidestep. More gallantly, such men might see seafarers' extramarital or paid sex as an unsuitable topic for 'lady' visitors. Yet the National Fishing Heritage Centre at Grimsby is setting a daring precedent with a new exhibition, Unsung Voices: The Role of Women in Our Deep Sea Fishing Communities. It records women's views of the relationship difficulties of men engaged in deep-sea fishing and touches on topics like domestic violence and family breakdown.

The problem is, of course, not only the absence of woman but her misrepresentations. Gaby Porter says of museums in general that 'where narratives and incidents or materials relating to women do not "fit" these ideals [of the feminine], they are couched in terms which show discomfort and unease: for example, where women worked in heavy and male-dominated industries. In these places, the terms of representation may become more sharply focused, shrill or humorous, or they may appear to deny woman and the feminine altogether, so that these have to be teased out from oblique references in other messages and materials.'[31] Maritime museums have exemplified such attitudes, mirroring the tensions that some men undoubtedly feel about women's presence on ships. Yet such tensions are the very stuff that public history can usefully address in order to open up ways of understanding women's connections with the sea.

Why does woman's absence matter?
Why does the absence of woman, and of gender relations, matter? It matters to me because I feel hurt, excluded, angry and confused when confronted by any omission of a history that I know exists. I assume that a public site of knowledge should show what I know from personal experience to be the case: that Britain's maritime history, if not yet its historiography, includes me and all the other women members of my seafaring family together with all the seafaring or sea-connected women I have interviewed or read about. If I do not

find that history in a public place that purports to be conveying maritime history then what do I make of that history and that place? What *else* might be missing and wrong? And why? The absence matters socially because a public service has an ethical duty to transmit information that shows a fair range of the many stories that are history: in this case, to show that our maritime past included both sexes. It also matters because it is psychically damaging to those 48–52 per cent of visitors who are women. It intensifies alienation if we fail to find ourselves. Using Lacanian theory, Gaby Porter argues that for women encountering the divide of subject/masculine and object/feminine – say at a museum – can mean a revisiting of that early gendered position which involves 'recognition of and subjection to an order in which she has no position in her own right, but only in relation to men.'[32] It disempowers and undermines women's confidence in their own ability and their right to be actively and validly engaged with the sea. Further, as Jones and Pay argue, 'theories and methodologies must be developed that incorporate the would as seen through women's eyes, rather than classifying their views as subjective and contrasting them with objective knowledge – a dichotomy between invalid subjective and invalid objective that cannot be accepted ...'[33]

Remembering is a form of constructive activity. Psychologist FC Bartlett argues it is 'not the retrieval of stored information, but the putting together of a claim about past states of affairs by means of a frame of shared cultural understanding.'[34] Kavanagh rightly suggests that when we go to museums 'even if we are not aware of it, we look for ourselves, for echoes of our own experiences, for identifiable things. By doing so, we are seeking the security of something we know before we can progress confidently to learn something new. If we can find nothing we recognise and little to engage our feelings, the learning potential of the exhibition is lost. In such circumstances, the chances are that our histories have been omitted and we are staring in the face of exclusion. In that eventuality, our own capacity for subversive history making may take over with old memories and stories brought forward to fill the gaps. If this too fails, all we are left with is a growing sense of absence and loss, a sense of history as death.'[35] No public service has the right to inflict that sense on any of its users. To fail to find ourselves matters both to our psychological well-being and to our learning – that learning with which we contribute to our society, including through the transmission of information to future generations (traditionally a key role for women as mothers and teachers of primary schoolchildren).Social scientist Alan Radley argues that 'museums, as with other edifices in the community (cathedrals, town halls, castles) are repositories of objects which exist as special artifacts, by reference to which past epochs may be read and understood. In these cases, people do not remember a series of personal events which touched their own lives but enjoy "a sense of the past" through the understanding of a history which other people appear to have created.'[36] The sense of the past offered by many maritime museums is akin to that offered by wartime propaganda films featuring heroic British Bulldogs.[37] It may be 'enjoyed' but is it ethical for public information services to offer a misleading experience (i.e. an orderly, masculine sea-conquering world without the chaos that 'woman' can represent) as a source of pleasure?

What is now being done?
Women and gender are increasingly on the agenda in maritime museums. There is more 'sea*farer*' and less 'sea*man*', even if there is still little 'sea*woman*' or discussion of their interfaces. We have reached the stage where internationally recognised maritime historian Frank Broeze can now say 'Naval history ... long regarded as a field of its own and largely the preserve of naval officers writing for professional and nationalistic purposes, is being modernized through a far more critical approach and a significant widening of its themes...'[38] Women's 'contribution signifies a resolute departure from the traditional and powerful patriarchy which controlled the subject in terms of staffing, publications and museum exhibitions...in many ways too, the new female maritime historians have emphasized the necessity of integrating maritime history into the historical mainstream.'[39] Maritime history has a very evident and growing sub-discipline – women's maritime history. And it offers scholarship on which exhibitions could be based, stimulated and focused through the establishing of a formal international electronic and paper forum for sharing: the Women and the Sea Network.

In this accelerated period of increasing women's maritime historiography there have been at least nine key events. The most noteworthy came from the museums and heritage world, not from academic history. They include:

1985 Hamburg Women's Waterfront History Project, Germany
1987 Women on the Docks Project, Second Chance to Learn, Liverpool, UK
1993 Women and the Sea Conference, Wellington Maritime Museum, NZ
1993 Women and the Sea Exhibition, Southampton Maritime Museum, UK
1995 What About Women: Our Place in Maritime History, exhibition at Australian National Maritime Museum, Sydney[40]
1996 Publication of seminal book on gender in the maritime world: *Iron Men, Wooden Women*. Eds M. Creighton and L. Norling.
1997 Women & the Sea Network established, National Maritime Museum, UK
1998 Frauen zur See seit 1945, exhibition at Flensburg Schiffsfahrt Museum, then touring, Germany
1999 Unsung Voices exhibition, National Fishing Heritage Centre, Grimsby UK

Why the change?
Why are maritime museums changing? Because of two major developments over the last few decades. Firstly, ordinary women and men are now represented in museums. This ties in with the ways sociology and labour studies have, in the past thirty years, begun a slow integration with academic maritime historiography.[41] Museums which once thought their job was only to display objects are now including people in their exhibitions. As maritime historian Malcolm Tull points out, 'the modern tendency is to see maritime history as now also concerned with shore-based people, institutions and facilities that make sea transport possible, as well as ships and the persons who sailed them.'[42] Secondly, women and other socially excluded groups have been inserted into museums generally, due to contemporary awareness about equal opportunities. Improvements instigated by WHAM! (Women in Heritage, Archives and Museums!)[43] parallel those of some impressively committed, gender-aware museum professionals at other

sites,[44] focusing for example on race and class. Feminist historiography in general has developed rapidly.[45] Women's maritime historiography is benefiting from its academic connection with gender history, women's history, oral history, community history and labour history, even if the focus is only slowly developing beyond the stage of saying 'women were there' to demonstrating what it *means* and *meant* that women were there.

Writers such as Joan Druett with her books on whaling women and Suzanne J. Stark on Royal Navy women have opened new doors.[46] This breakthrough in women's maritime historiography builds on work done over the past fifty years. Initially the information about women at sea was sparse, text-based, read through masculine lenses and usually focused on isolated exceptions, non-contextualised women such as pirate Mary Read, or cross-dressers like Ann Talbot and Hannah Snell. Early writers included Edward Rowe Snow, John Carlova, and Basil Greenhill,[47] who collaborated with Ann Giffard, probably the first British women maritime historian of women. As part of that history of women's contribution, museums have become increasingly unable to ignore women, if not gender relations. This shift is helped by changes in personnel. Kavanagh reports that a key factor in the transition in museums generally is 'the deep personal commitment to be found among social history curators no longer prepared to tolerate exclusions, especially where gender is concerned.'[48] Women and progressive people who became museum professionals in the 1970s are now in a position of influence and beginning to outnumber older traditional colleagues. They can instate that which they notice is absent and insert not just women but gender, with all the hegemonic overturnings that creates.

That change has been more difficult to effect in maritime museums, which have tended to remain strongholds of the blue-blazer brigade, resistant both to women's presence and to innovative notions of cultural historiography. For example, Mary-Louise Williams describes the process by which the Australia National Maritime Museum decided to stop calling the ships 'she'. 'I had no idea that this rather innocuous proposal would cause the heated debates and affront that it was to attract....[including a pencilled comment] "P. C. Femonazis" – which I took to roughly translate as "politically correct female monsters" which ... seemed a cry from the heart from someone who seemed to be repelling some mythological attack.'[49] Moreover, changes in museum interpretation practice now mean that objects and absences are questioned and challenged. This provides, for example, opportunities for labels asking visitors where they think women were quartered on that ship, or why women weren't there. A further explanation is the simple economic need for survival. Higher visitor numbers are needed. Janet Owens of the National Maritime Museum says, 'The redisplay of galleries and opening of new galleries earlier this year was part of an attempt to "feminise" the museum; to make it more appealing to women and children by adding more human elements to the history of the sea. Early indications are that this has been successful with the target audience, and the museum will continue to monitor carefully the results of future surveys to continue this trend.' [50]

Conclusion
To turn 'sea*men*' into 'peoples of the maritime community' is to put the 'whole' in 'history', to state the multiplicities necessary for principled historiography and public history. We need to connect woman/man, sea/land, object/subject – and then explore. Learning and teaching about women's maritime history means a future with exhibits that go behind and beyond gendered stereotypes. We do not need the myth of Jill ashore, probably pregnant, weeping for her big brave Jack Tar who is out there fighting the typhoons, mermaids, litigious American passengers and using the big ship's computer that her little noddle wouldn't understand. The growth of my own knowledge about women pirates and my stewardessing Aunty May's peculiar job have revealed important truths to me about women's history that refute old fallacies. I discovered that stewardessing was the way enterprising working-class girls managed to see the world and that piracy was not about Errol Flynn-style glamour. It is knowledge of Aunty May and her sisters and the sea that enables me to know and tell[51] the more organic truth: that these seafarers were people like me. In Kavanagh's terms, I can recognise myself in their stories just as women may be able recognise themselves in the deliberately created new galleries and exhibitions from Grimsby to Sydney and Greenwich to San Francisco. Tourism theorist John Urry points out that 'within cultural analysis, metaphors of travel, or narratives and home and displacement, of borders

and crossings, have become exceptionally widespread. Deleuze employs the metaphor of the nomadic subject; others of cultures of being "on the road" (a kind of "Easy Rider" view of culture).'[52] We might apply concepts from cultural studies notions to probe, with a gender-aware lens, the personal and popular meanings of the sea, sea-related work, those women and men who traverse it and those who operate on its borders.

Above all, there remains to be explored that special tension between the sea as site of Otherness and the ship as site of not only the familiar, but the transported, rigidly codified mores of land in which woman is lesser and Other. We might see the ship in cultural theorist Jacques Derrida's terms, as a borderland where woman is especially troubling to the masculine. If she, in her frocks, with her babies, can be on ship then doesn't this deny that seafaring requires solely masculine traits? If she can exist in this Other place then does she thereby imply that masculinity is unnecessary or a fiction? Gaby Porter found in exhibitions that 'women and the feminine become, literally, the frontiers by which space and knowledge are defined: they are the more distant and precise elements, in the background and at the edges of the picture.' [53] Without that particular presence, how would men's maritime history then be seen? And how does women's position at the background and on the edges help us understand the whole story of gender and the sea?

Notes
1 Sally Fodie, *Waitemata Ferry Tales*, illustrations by Jim Storey, Ferry Boat Publishers, Auckland, New Zealand, 1995. Thanks to Jim and Sally for permission to publish these pictures.
2 The 'devil's ballast' was what women, even the queen, were called when on ship in Shakespeare's *Pericles*. The superstitious seafarers believed that to jettison representatives of half the human race, even if this one was a queen, would allay a storm.
3 Pierre Bourdieu, *The Field of Cultural Production*, Polity, Cambridge, 1993, p. 298.
4 Some aspects of this definition were taken from Fiona Mclean, 'Services Marketing: The Case for Museums', *The Services Industries Journal*, vol 14, no 2, April 1994, London, pp. 190–191.
5 Sian Jones and Sharon Pay, 'The Legacy of Eve,' in Peter Gathercole and David Lowenthal,(eds), *The Politics of the Past*, Unwin Hyman, London, 1990, p. 160.
6 Mary-Louise Williams, 'Out of Sight – Out of Mind: Women's Place in Maritime Museums,' *Proceedings : IXth International Congress of Maritime Museums*, (eds.), Adrian Jarvis, Roger Knight and Michael Stammers, National Maritime Museum and Merseyside Maritime Museum, London and Liverpool.

7   Women's presence on ships has often been unofficial, therefore unrecorded. For data showing a detailed breakdown of British women seafarers' presence at sea, see especially table 1 in my 'The Company of Women', *The Northern Mariner/Le Marin du nord*, IX, no 2, April 1999, pp. 69–86. Today women are 6.3% of officers and 8.4% of ratings in the Royal Navy, according to the MOD, Oct 1999, phone interview.
8   Stanley, 'The Company of Women.' p. 70–71.
9   Margaret S Creighton and Lisa Norling, (eds.), *Iron Men, Wooden Women: Gender and Seafaring in the Atlantic World, 1700-1920*, Johns Hopkins Press, Baltimore and London, 1996.
10 Gaby Porter, 'Seeing through solidity: a feminist perspective on museums' in *Theorizing Museums*, eds Sharon Macdonald and Gordon Fyfe, Blackwell, Oxford, 1996, p. 105.
11 I am grateful to Rachel Mulhearn at Merseyside Maritime Museum for her ideas about Jill Tar, as well as generous help on early drafts of this article.
12 *Signals Mail Order*, home shopping catalogue from the Royal Naval Museum and HMS Victory, Portsmouth, 1999.
13 Robert Hewison, *The Heritage Industry: Britain in a Climate of Decline*, Methuen, 1987, p. 146.
14 Cynthia Enloe, *Does Khaki become you?* Pluto Press, London, 1983.
15 Henry William Flayhart III, 'Ocean Historiography,' in Frank Broeze (ed) *Research in Maritime History: Maritime History at the Crossroads: a critical review of recent historiography*, Research in Maritime History no 9, Maritime Economic History Association, St John's, Newfoundland, 1995, p. 275.
16 David Williams, 'The Progress of Maritime History', *Journal of Transport History*, xiv, no 2, Sept 1993, p. 29.
17 Fuller details of systematic survey I did are given in a paper for the Maritime Heritage conference, Carried Along by the Currents? University of Portsmouth, April 1999. I am grateful to the organisers Ann Day and Ken Lunn for the exciting questions in their positional paper, which spurred me to frame my thoughts in this particular way.
18 Hewison, *The Heritage Industry*, p. 137.
19 Campbell McMurray, 'The Maritime Museum: its place in the changing world', Peter Davies Memorial Lecture given at Merseyside Maritime Museum, May 29 1997.
20 Emailed data from Janet Owens, NMM, November 1999.
21 Robert Hewison refers to 'that distance when memory softens and sweetens. But there is no need for personal nostalgia. Here [meaning at Beamish] the displays do it for you,' Hewison, p. 95. Similarly the Emma exhibits recall a time when men were allegedly not only great military and naval heroes but great lovers too.
22 I found fourteen out of eighteen galleries were closed for renovation, therefore my survey was only partial.
23 Emailed data from Janet Owens, NMM, November 1999.
24 Phone interview with Averil Scott, Marketing Dept, NMM, Oct 1999.
25 Mary-Louise Williams, 'Out of Sight – Out of Mind', p. 118–119.
26 Susan Pearce, *Museums, Objects and Collections, a cultural study*, Leicester University Press, Leicester, 1992, p. 63.
27 Jones and Pay, 'The legacy of Eve', p. 162.
28 Gaby Porter, 'Seeing Through Solidity', p. 111.
29 Gaynor Kavanagh 'Looking for Ourselves, Inside and Outside Museums,' *Gender and History*, vol 6, no 3, November 1994, pp. 370–371.

30 Ibid, p. 374.
31 Porter, 'Seeing Through Solidity,' p. 113.
32 Porter, 'Seeing Through Solidity,' p. 11.
33 Jones and Pay, 'The Legacy of Eve', p. 165.
34 Alan Radley, 'Artifacts, Memory and a Sense of the Past', in David Middleton and Derek Edwards (eds), *Collective Remembering*, Sage London, Newbury Park and New Delhi, 1990, p. 46, citing psychologist F.C. Barlett, *Remembering: A Study in Experimental and Social Psychology*, Cambridge University Press, Cambridge, 1932.
35 Kavanagh, 'Looking for Ourselves', p. 374.
36 Radley, 'Artifacts, Memory and a Sense of the Past', p. 47.
37 For example, The Cruel Sea, 1952, starring Jack Hawkins.
38 Frank Broeze, *Research in Maritime History: Maritime History at the Crossroads*, p. xiv.
39 Ibid, p. xvii.
40 Mary Louise Williams, 'Out of Sight – Out of Mind,' pp. 121–122.
41 Key historians in the process include Marcus Rediker and Eric Sager. The initiative came with Jesse Lemisch's seminal article, 'Jack Tar in the Streets: merchant seamen in the politics of revolutionary America', *William and Mary Quarterly*, 3rd ser., 25, July 1968, pp. 371–407 and the Working Men Who Got Wet conference, Newfoundland, 1980.
42 Malcolm Tull, 'Maritime History in Australia', in Broeze, *Research in Maritime History: Maritime History at the Crossroads*, p. 3.
43 Women in Heritage, Archives and Museums. Membership Secretary Margaret Brooks, Sound Archive, Imperial War Museum, London.
44 For example the Museum of London's Peopling of London exhibition, an anti-racist initiative.
45 For example, the Women's History Network has quadrupled in size in seven years and there are journals such as *Gender and History* and *Women's History Review*.
46 Joan Druett: *'She Was a Sister Sailor': The Whaling Journals of Mary Brewster*, 1845–1851, Mystic, Connecticut, 1992. This won the North American Society for Oceanic History prize for best non-naval book published that year. *Petticoat Whalers: whaling wives at sea 1820–1920*, Collins, Auckland, New Zealand, 1991. *Hen Frigates: wives of merchant captains under sail*, Simon and Schuster, New York, 1998. See also Suzanne J. Stark 'Two Women Whalers,' *American Neptune* Winter 1984; *Female Tars: women aboard ship in the age of sail*, Naval Institute Press, Annapolis, Maryland, 1996; 'Mates at Sea: Nineteenth Century New England Captain's Wives', *Seaport Magazine,* New York, Spring 1986.
47 Edward Rowe Snow, *Women of the Sea*, New York,1962; John Carlova, *Mistress of the Seas*, Dodd, Mead, New York, 1964; and Basil Greenhill, particularly his work with Ann Giffard, *Women under Sail: Letters and Journals concerning eight women travelling or working in sailing vessels between 1829 and 1949*, Great Albion Books, South Brunswick, 1971. Linda Grant DePauw, *Seafaring Women*, Houghton Mifflin, Boston, 1982 has a thorough bibliography.
48 Kavanagh, 'Looking for Ourselves', p. 370.
49 Mary Louise Williams, 'Out of Sight – Out of Mind', p. 120.
50 Janet Owens, NMM, email, November 1999.
51 For example, on pirates, *Bold in her Breeches, Women Pirates Across the Ages*, Pandora, London, 1996; on nurses; 'All at Sea', *Nursing Times*, vol 94,

no 8, Feb 25 1998, cover and pp. 28–30; on women captains; 'Women Taking the Helm', *Maritime Heritage*, Nov–Dec 1998, vol 2.4; on seagoing liner typists; 'Finding a brief flowering of typists at sea: evidence from a new Cunard deposit', *Business archives Sources and History*, no 76, Nov 1998; on stewardesses; 'The Company of Women: stewardesses on inter-war liners', paper given to the Canadian Nautical Research Society conference, Canada, June 1998 and *The Northern Mariner/Le Marin du nord*, IX, no 2, April 1999, pp. 69–86; 'Bad girls booted off liners: stewardesses' careers 1919–39', paper given to McQuisack Seminar, QMW, University of London, June 1998; on laundresses; 'Washing dirty linen in public: laundering for Cunard and White Star Liners, 1900–1938', *Liverpool Yearbook 1999*, (forthcoming).
52 John Urry, 'How societies remember the past', in Macdonald and Fyfe, 'Theorizing Museums,' p. 57. Urry is referring to Giles Deleuze, 'Nomad Thought' in D. Allison (ed.), *The New Nietzsche*, Delta, New York, 1977.
53 Porter, 'Seeing Through Solidity,' p. 112.

Language and landscape

The construction of place in an East London borough

Bruce Wheeler

Introduction

Newham is a place. It has a physical existence, something that can be measured and categorised; an apparently objective presence that can be defined in terms of its geology, topography, climate and population. It exists within geographical and administrative boundaries and in its spatial relationship to other places. It is a place on the map, a place on many maps, each of which have a different purpose. But it is there – a thing we can travel to and from and within.

As a *place*, however, it is more than the mere collection of its physical parts. It has a social and cultural form, an identity, or more properly a collection of contesting identities, that have changed and are changing. Newham, like its eleventh–century predecessor 'Hamme', or the later County Boroughs of East and West Ham,[1] has meanings, both evolved and constructed, geographical and historical, products of the dialectic between space and time. It is a place of people: a place of plans, possibilities, values and beliefs, pasts, presents and futures. Newham in this sense, like any other place, is essentially a construction; fabricated on the ground and fashioned in the mind; built in space and built in time. It has a physical existence, and an existence in the minds of people. To concentrate solely on one aspect would be to ignore much of its substance and to grasp only a fragment of its totality.

Language

Language is a system of symbolic representation. Names describe, locate and give meaning. They are the link between the descriptor and the described, the locator and the location, the 'meaner' and the meant: in short a medium of exchange. Language is problematic in as much as it is never neutral and possesses its own structures that can condition both its users and that to which it is applied. But that having been said, the analysis of language is central in any history of representations. As a medium it provides a point of access to the social realities and mentalities of the individuals and societies who employ it. By engaging with these subjective representations, by constructing a history of verbal formations in which language, as metaphor and symbol, is examined precisely as metaphor and symbol, the historian is freed: 'the source no longer screens historians from the reality they are trying to recapture, it even becomes a transparent object.'[2] The subjectivity of these sources is a given, they become 'useful' historical sources when they are relocated back into the social structures from which they emanate.

Names are important. They are not merely words on a map designating physical location or topographical features, they serve to encapsulate the total idea of a place and are saturated with meaning and value. They have an ideological dimension: through the change of St Petersburg to Petrograd, to Leningrad, and back to St Petersburg, we can trace shifting political positions. Dyfed or Pembrokeshire, Humberside or the East Riding, Ulster or the Six Counties, each articulates an identity and defines a community. Place names can have a more ephemeral cultural resonance: the 'Swinging London' of the 1960s, repackaged in today's 'Cool Britannia'. A suburb in one epoch can be part of the inner city in the next and carries the baggage of imagery that such terms attract. Just as pertinent in this case are the representations implicit in ideas like the East End or Thames Gateway, brownfield sites and heritage landscapes. The manipulation of names can change perceived value: in the 1980s Surrey Docks station on the London Underground was changed to Surrey Quays. Names are powerful signifiers; their existence and the changes they undergo reflect and inform the wider spheres in which they exist. Taken together over time they can read almost like an autobiography of place, written collectively by the people and the societies from which they emanate, preserving themes and memories, identities and histories in the aspic of language and meaning.

The academic discipline of toponymy, the study of place

names, is in many ways still trapped in the world of nineteenth-century philology; a specialised adjunct of professional history. In Britain it has most often been used, alongside archaeology, to map the migration and settlement patterns of different linguistic groupings and reconstruct the environment of the distant past; a form of study that seldom leaves the confines of the university library or map room. This approach, consisting largely of the cataloguing and classification of toponyms, runs the risk once the event and origin of the naming are identified, of losing sight of the historical significance of subsequent change. It can also mask the fact that historic names were conscious constructions; and, that once in place, they continue to have an effect, resonating on and from the societies that have and continue to utilise them in ordering the landscape. 'As if, above all, the meaning of a word were influenced more by its own past than by the contemporary state of the vocabulary which, in its turn, is determined by the social conditions of the moment.'[3]

As condensations of meaning place names remain a powerful referential tool in any work of history. In a geographical history, looking at humanity in its environment over time, place names offer a quick and accessible entry point to the processes of cultural construction. In their role as the binding agents in the creation of geosocial identities, their significance becomes even more apparent. We can trace their influence in ordering our present, and the present's role in navigating, mapping and constructing the past.

The creation of Newham, which was formed in 1965 by amalgamating the old County Boroughs of East and West Ham, is a prime example of the power of the etymological discourse reworking the past and legitimating the present. Newham was a completely new name, a repackaging of the 'Hamme' which appeared in the Domesday Book. As the Edwardian local historian Dr Pagenstecher commented: 'East Ham, as its name implies, lies in the east of West Ham, on the outer confines of Greater London ... originally it formed with West Ham one parish which went by the common name of Ham. It is not until 1181–2 that the distinction of East and West Ham occurs.'[4] No doubt the committees responsible for devising the new name in the 1960s were influenced by this historicist current. The hoped for unity of the new was transplanted from the perceived unity of the old. Old 'Hamme' was reborn in New 'Ham'. Newham became a place, it had a genealogical heritage. As a unitary authority, it had a unitary, instead of a fragmentary, past. Three decades later no one can doubt that it exists, that it is there.

The place
On the edge of London, from its earliest beginnings the area we now know as Newham lay on a frontier. In the Middle Ages it was a centre for processing the agricultural produce of the eastern counties for onward transportation to the City. Later, its docks and railway hub performed the same function, but this time not just for London and its domestic hinterland. In the nineteenth and twentieth centuries it mediated between an imperial metropolis and its colonies. It became a gateway, a point of entry and departure.

This frontier function was not just limited to the economic and physical. It became a staging post, a 'Custom House' in both senses of the word; a nexus for exchanging cultures as well as cargoes; a home for migrating peoples and their ideas. West Ham and East Ham were Victorian boom towns. In the last quarter of the nineteenth century they exhibited the highest rate of population increase anywhere in the country. Their exponential industrial growth drew in new inhabitants from all over Britain and the world, giving rise to new settlements, contemporary frontier towns, on the virgin territory of the Thames-side marshes. Throughout the twentieth century the process has continued. In the 1920s West Ham had one of the largest black populations in Britain. In the 1990s the area has one of the largest and most diverse ethnic make-ups in the country, if not the world. These new peoples and modes of production have brought new ideas, new tensions and challenges. At the cutting edge, it formed a political frontier. From the silk-workers of the 1670s, through the dissenting radicals and Quakers of the eighteenth century to the 'New Unions' and municipal socialism of the nineteenth and early twentieth centuries, the area has been infused with this dynamic discourse. At the end of the twentieth century it is the pace and scale of its industrial and supposed social decay that has in many ways come to monopolise its public representation.

New names for old villages

The parish of East Ham comprises several hamlets, viz.: Wall End, Manor Park and Plashet. The latter, which until recently was a small rural village, has grown to a busy little town, since the London, Tilbury and Southend Railway have established a station there, under the name of Upton Park.

Katherine Fry, 1888.[5]

The little shops were convenient but most food was bought from the stalls in Stratford market or Queens Road, Upton Park. Though miles apart, my mother would walk the length of both markets, seeking to stretch her meagre budget by buying for a halfpenny cheaper.

John Gorman, 1995.[6]

Katherine Fry lived in a place she called Plashet. She refers to it constantly in the pages of her history of the local area as she does to the neighbouring hamlet of Upton. These were distinct localities. In the still largely rural landscape of the mid-nineteenth century they would have been easily distinguishable; rather than houses, there would have been fields in between. John Gorman's mother shopped in a place she called Upton Park. In purely physical terms she was walking the same ground as her predecessor, but by the 1930s the physical and social environment was completely altered. It was, as the name change signifies, a different *place*. Industrialisation, urbanisation, and the countless lives lived in between had effectively redrawn the map. Both places were now part of a greater London. A new series of relationships and meanings had recast the terrain in popular imagination. The landscapes of Plashet and Upton, semi-rural hamlets punctuated by large country houses, where the leisured mercantile class relaxed away from the tensions of the metropolis, had been replaced by an urban working-class vista.

Today there is no Plashet as such. There is a Plashet School, a Plashet Cemetery, Plashet Park, Plashet Grove and Plashet Road. It is also a local government ward, a part of the London Borough of Newham. However, on most other levels, say as a destination on a bus route, it has disappeared. On an everyday level Plashet no longer exists. Just as the material traces of the people who named it and inhabited it in the past are hidden by later deposits, as the Mrs Gormans succeed the Miss Frys, the name itself has been buried beneath an accre-

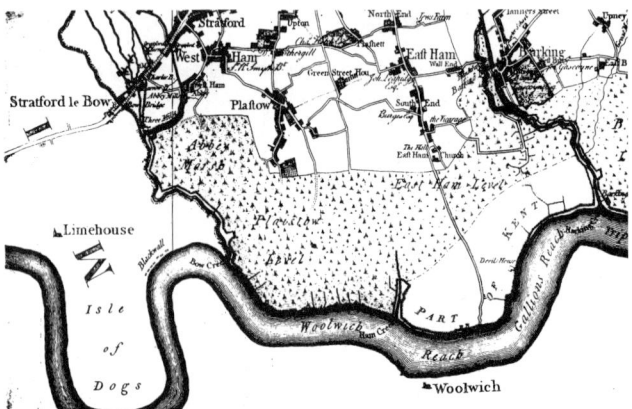

Extract from Chapman and André's Map of the County of Essex, 1777.

tion of new meanings, ideas and memories. We inhabit the same spaces, but the places, giving meaning to and drawing significance from their names, and the times, have changed. Likewise Upton is now just another ward name, though it was undoubtedly a place until relatively recently. Today it has been colonised and subsumed by the more recent entities of Upton Park to the south and Forest Gate to the north. A glance through the property pages of the local newspaper, the *Newham Recorder*, reinforces this picture (See Appendix 1). Upton, like Plashet, is no longer a place that anybody really lives in. As ideas, as *imagined communities*, their time has long gone.

This transformation of place names is symptomatic of the changing social, economic and political landscape that these names order and define. While it is hardly surprising that new places, new buildings and neighbourhoods need names, what is striking in this context is the rapidity with which new toponyms have come to obliterate their antecedents. Such a change can only be permanent when the inhabitants of any locality, accept and utilise new names in their day-to-day lives. Whether we call it capitalism, industrialisation or modernity, this is a powerful process, dislocating and remoulding lives and communities just as it recasts and refunctionalises the physical landscape. The disappearance of

Upton and Plashet are just two examples of this trend. Their existence as geographical entities was to a large extent the result of their economic, social and political significance. As these changed so did their names. They were places on the map because the map makers, publishers and users accepted their importance. As eighteenth century sources such as Rocque's *Survey of London* (1746), and Chapman and André's maps of Essex (1777) demonstrate, Upton and Plashet did exist in the pre-industrial topography. In both cases their significance came from the fact that they were the homes of the local 'great and good', whose houses are identified on the map. These maps had a clear social construction – the space was ordered largely in relation to its elite inhabitants, the rest of the population was anonymous. A hundred or so years later they too had disappeared.

Changing functions: a modern world

The building of the railways from the 1830s was the first piece in the jigsaw of Newham's modern development. In its initial phase the emerging railway infrastructure was important to the growth of industry within the borough and the demand for labour that accompanied it. This phenomenon can be most clearly traced in relation to the south of the borough, in particular the development and growth of Canning Town, Custom House, Silvertown and Beckton, and the industrial areas of Stratford and West Ham in the north-west. The railway was also important in the growth of the rest of the borough, although there was a significant time lag between the railways' construction, starting in the 1830s, and the mainly residential developments which characterise the north and north-east around Forest Gate, Upton Park, East Ham and Manor Park, the vast bulk of which occurred between 1870 and 1914. In terms of actual house building, and the social landscape that it accommodated, the process was gradual. This rough north/south and residential/industrial demarcation can be discerned in the local toponymy.

The North: salubrious streets

The coming of the railways was pivotal in the social homogenisation of individual neighbourhoods and suburbs, leading to the increasing segregation of the area along class lines. Generally this is one of the most salient characteristics of Victorian urbanisation. Improved transport meant those who could afford it no longer had to live in the immediate vicinity of their workplace. This led to the increasing polarisation of communities and the development of largely single class neighbourhoods. In London the growth of these new districts was stimulated by the 1864 Cheap Trains Act. As Roy Porter comments:

... from the 1870s the railway brought something quite new: the working-class suburb, thanks to the 1864 Cheap Trains Act, with the idea of the workmen's fare ... this encouraged speculative builders to provide housing for the respectable working classes in railway suburbs in districts unlikely to attract the better class of commuter. North-east and east London were particularly affected. From the 1870s stations in Tottenham, Walthamstow, Leyton, West Ham, Plaistow, Upton Park, Manor Park and similar districts became surrounded by endless files of regimented, plain two- and three-storey terraces, whose occupants were typically skilled artisans, policemen and firemen, railway engineers or gaffers in the gasworks, men with the security and income to allow them to rent or even buy a place of their own a half-hour train ride from work.[7]

Many of the area's new residents represented the success stories of the era, escaping the 'residuum' and 'abyss' of the old East End a couple of miles to the west across the River Lea. As John Gorman recounts in another autobiographical excerpt, about a couple who lodged with his family in the 1930s in nearby Stratford: 'When Sarah, who came from Blackstone Street, Bow Common, told her family that she was moving to Stratford, they thought it was "very posh", and that she had done very well for herself.'[8] For Henry Jaques, a shirtmaker from Bow, the motives for his move to Forest Gate in 1877 are slightly more practical but still belie the links between fresh air and social status:

The health of my dear ones and of the children was such that it was put into my heart to try and arrange to remove to a suburb of London. The doctor was always in the house to one or another and, after mature thought and prayer, it was ultimately resolved that we should look for a house away from these dense districts.

Very many families were leaving the district for the more salubrious air of Leytonstone and Forest Gate. These two Hamlets then were little more than villages. We were led to seek a house in the latter locality. It seemed a very gigantic business, but when once we were resolved the matter was followed up, and eventually we decided upon a small house at 28 Bignold

Rd. at a rent of £28 per annum, where we removed in July 1877 and thus began our connexion with Forest Gate which was destined to be both happy and lasting.[9]

In the case of Upton Park we can observe a similar cultural construction of the area as a healthier and more socially desirable alternative to the cramped conditions of the old East End. The name itself was originally used to designate a new, and relatively small, residential housing development in Upton, to the east of the recently opened West Ham Park.[10] The highlighting of this amenity in the place name was clearly a means of raising the tone of the area, attaching cachet to what in many ways was just another grid of late-Victorian terraces. With the appropriate marketing strategy this imagery was always likely to increase the social standing and with it the financial value of adjacent properties. The 'Park' attribution in many late-Victorian urban developments connotes that peculiar *rus in urbe* sentiment even now such a potent cultural metaphor. The name was clearly designed to promote a particular image, immediately familiar to the respectable working-class tenant, attracting the upwardly mobile artisans, foremen and clerks of the era with the promise of a suburban dream: self-contained family houses, a patch of garden, respectable neighbours and orderly streets. As the urban historian H.J. Dyos commented, these suburban dreams 'might almost have been written into the genetic code of the ordinary people whose great-grandparents had in so many cases left the country to join the town.'[11]

This theme of urbanised rusticity can be read in the choice of numerous street names in the area such as Vale, Sylvan, Oakdale, Ferndale, Rosedale and Birchdale Roads. The use of 'park' is also popular, most obviously in Park Road and Park Grove, and slightly more creatively in Ham Park, Caistor Park, Matthews Park and Margery Park Roads. The areas of Woodgrange Park and Manor Park to the east are yet further variations on this basic theme. The utilisation of 'Gardens' is another. Cotswold, Chesley, Montpelier, Henniker, Geoffrey and Cheltenham Gardens on East Ham's Central Park Estate, still for Newham an upmarket location, are the best examples.

On some levels the Victorian park itself can be read as a hankering after a rural pre-industrial and pre-modern past. However, their actual design, surrounded by railings and gates, and with carefully delineated areas for specific functions, belies the fact that they were essentially just as manufactured and ordered as the factories, shops and offices whose inhabitants they were set up for. Parks were more generally part of the 'rational recreation' movement of the late nineteenth century. With the public baths, libraries and museums, which appeared alongside them, they were a means of enticing working people out of pubs, music halls and other dens of vice and slothfulness, to spend their time on more 'profitable' and 'respectable' pursuits. The landscape was increasingly mapped in terms of its moral geography. New spaces with new names were engineered to contain or exclude social ills, controlling behaviour through the production of healthy places for healthy minds and bodies. In the dominant discourse of the late nineteenth century, the age of social hygiene, moral and physical health were indistinguishable.

Slightly further to the south and bordering Plaistow lay the Upton Manor estate, developed earlier during the 1860s. Its name can also be seen as cashing in on the respectable and gentrified image of the area by referencing itself within the same context as the country house estates of the mercantile elite who had inhabited the area in its pre-industrial past. While Upton itself was a respectable idealised community, the new suffixes seem to be designed to create new exclusivities and boundaries within the overall respectable suburban image. Upton Manor, now subsumed into a larger Upton Park, only survives today in the name of the Upton Manor Tavern on Plashet Road. To the north, the new suburb of Forest Gate echoed the same design. Although its name is slightly older and possesses at least some historical antecedence, it too became part of a constructed image. The name itself derives from a gate erected on the road across the Wanstead Flats, then as now, part of Epping Forest, to stop cattle straying off the grazing land. The name does not appear on either the Rocque or Chapman and Andre maps, suggesting that its later choice as the railway station name, and subsequent expansion to cover the area that it now does, can be interpreted in the same light as the other urban/rustic appellations. It might equally have been named Wanstead Slip, a less fashionable toponym that was applied to part of the area as late as 1899.[12] The area's most exclusive streets on the Woodgrange Estate, built in the 1870s and consisting of a grid of leafy avenues, were named after royal country residences: Windsor,

Osborne, Hampton, Balmoral, Claremont and Sandringham. In this context the double-fronted detached Victorian Villas that lined them attempt to reflect the image the street names incorporate; they were almost literally, in the discourse of the age, little palaces.

The South: company towns

In the year 1850 Silvertown did not exist, and West Ham was a small and practically unknown suburban district in the east of London, with barely 18,000 inhabitants. In 1900 Silvertown has the population of a fairly large country town and West Ham ... boasts some 300,000 inhabitants, being the eighth largest town in England, and exceeding the population of several European capitals.[13]

Prior to the 1850s the southern portion of the borough consisted of marsh land, seasonally flooded, only used as rough grazing for cattle, horses and pigs. As both the Rocque and Chapman and Andre maps indicate, there were no settlements in this area and as a result no place names south of Plaistow. This featureless, and thus practically anonymous, expanse of land was designated the East Ham and Plaistow levels. By the end of the nineteenth century industry had transformed the landscape, and with it the toponymy, in one of the most rapid and comprehensive developments that had ever been witnessed. For the contemporary Victorian commentator these 'changes, perhaps unequalled in the history of any other portion of the United Kingdom',[14] were an awe-inspiring spectacle. The Thames and Lea-side marshes had, in little more than a generation, mutated into a vast industrial complex. This area had become significant; it had a substance – it too was now a *place*.

The banks of the lower Lea around Stratford had long been an industrial and manufacturing centre. The processing of agricultural produce from the eastern counties, flour milling, bread baking, slaughtering and tanning, for onward sale to London, had been an important element in the local economy throughout the medieval period. In the late sixteenth century textile industries appeared, particularly silk weaving and later calico printing. Stratford was also notable for gunpowder production, paper manufacture, distilling and ceramics. It was from the mid-nineteenth century that the mass industrialisation of the area really took off.

If the railway provided the initial spur for development, the next impetus was the passage in 1854 of the Metropolitan Building Act, which sought to curtail noxious and toxic industries from operating within the London area. West Ham, which lay on the east bank of the river Lea, then in Essex, was exempt from these restrictions and was the prime site for the establishment of these industrial processes which at the time included: 'distilleries, breweries, chemical and dye works, print-works, jute spinning mills, manufactures of vestas and matches, printing ink, aniline colour, varnish, soap and candle factories, oil, grease, creosote, bone-boiling, paraffin, coprolite, nitro-phosphate, guano, and other artificial manure and gas and tar works.'[15] As the construction industry's trade journal, *The Builder*, commented of West Ham in 1886:

Half a century ago it was a straggling village and ... might have remained so but for the Act of 1854, which placed many ... restrictions on the manufactories existing within the metropolis. Their owners naturally sought a retreat where nobody could interfere with them and found, at West Ham ... liberty to make smells and generally pollute the atmosphere, cheap land, and proximity to water carriage. So West Ham increased rapidly and became one of the busiest and dirtiest places in the kingdom.[16]

The development of the world's largest gasworks at Beckton, in neighbouring East Ham, by the Gas, Light and Coke Company from 1870, was another major component in the areas rapid industrial growth. The opening of the Northern Outfall Sewer in the 1860s, which terminated at Beckton's massive sewage works, then the largest in Europe, confirmed the areas status as London's waste processing centre. As part of this project the monumental Abbey Mills pumping station designed by Joseph Bazalgette, which opened in 1868, was dubbed the 'temple of effluvium' and 'cathedral of sewage'. It became both a landmark for the area and a visual epithet for the age, embodying an ambivalence towards modernity; a way of sanitising and re-ordering the disorder that rapid industrialisation was then creating, as it destroyed and reconstituted so much of the contemporary social and physical fabric of the era.[17]

The modern city was unpleasant, unruly and unhygienic but at the same time a source of awe, pride and wonder. James Thorne, describing Plaistow in his *Handbook to the Environs of London*, paints a familiar picture:

> Unpleasant manufacturies, driven from the capital, have settled down in the Marshes. The great Metropolitan Sewer, in the form of a huge grass covered embankment, has been carried across the level, and through the vill. The construction of the sewer, the opening of the rly., and the proximity of the great manufacturing establishments caused a large influx of the labouring classes. The gentry migrated ... The trees have been felled; the fields, changed into streets which lead nowhere, are left unfinished and fragmentary, and lined with mean little tenements ... dirty, frail and gardenless...The old vill has extended into Barking Road, and spread out over the marshes, and been met by the straggling streets and houses from Hall Ville, Silver Town, Canning Town and the Victoria Docks, manufacturing and shipping quarters ... grown up within the last few years about the great docks, chemical, creosoting, artificial manure, engineering and various other works, without order and without oversight; are dirty, incomplete, unfragrant, unattractive, but in many points of view exceedingly interesting.[18]

The other major component in Newham's industrial development was the opening of the Royal Victoria Dock in 1855. This was followed by the Royal Albert in 1880 and the King George V in 1921. Between them they formed a massive shipping centre, the largest, in terms of water frontage and cargo volume, deepest, and most modern in the world. With the other industries that grew up alongside them they created the massive demand for labour that led to the phenomenal population increases of the era. In turn whole new districts were established to house the new workers around the docks and the factories.

As most of these industries relied almost exclusively on casual labourers, for whom public transport was financially out of reach, and because of 'the strong imperative to be part of a community which knew when work was available',[19] these new townships were clustered around the docks and manufacturing areas, squeezed between the factories, works and waterfronts. As Dr Pagenstecher commented in his local history of 1909:

> The greater part of the marshes between Plaistow and the Thames have been absorbed by the three townships of Hallsville, Canning Town and Silvertown ... The whole district is a collection of industries ... There are hardly any well to do people living in the district, as there is no attraction to keep those in residence who can afford to get away. It is a purely working class community, and since the docks attract far more men than can possibly be employed, the number of unskilled labourers keeps rising year by year.[20]

The toponymy of south Newham echoes its function. Tidal Basin[21] and Custom House took their names directly from the industrial landscape that gave rise to them. The other new settlements, developed by the industrial elite, drew their names from the same source. George Canning, one of the chief engineers of the Victoria Dock, gave his name to Canning Town: the 'Hall' of Hallsville was a director of the Thames Ironworks, Shipbuilding & Engineering Company; Silvertown drew its name from the india rubber, waterproofing and insulating material manufacturers, S.W. Silver & Co; and the 'Beck' in Beckton was the Governor of the Gas, Light and Coke Company. These were quite literally company towns; their names exemplifying a crystallisation of the industrialists' hegemony, saturating the local geography. It would have been hard to escape their influence. In the 1890s, a worker could reside in Tate Road, go to evening classes at the Tate Institute, take a stroll around Lyle Park, before returning to the sugar refinery for the next shift. In the 1990s the only difference would be that the Institute would provide refreshment of a liquid rather than cerebral nature, having been re-endowed as a community centre and social club in the 1960s.

These and similarly derived names litter the surrounding streets. Bidder, Peto and Stephenson were all contractors on the Victoria Dock construction. The 'Cooks' of Cooks Road were factory owners; Knights Road drew its name from the soap manufacturers John Knight Ltd and Normandy Terrace from the Normandy Patent and Marine Aerated Freshwater Company. The Thames Ironworks provided many of the pre-cast sections of Brunel's Avon and Menai Straits bridges and the engineer's name was given to the street in Canning Town. Henley was a director of the Telegraph and Cable works in North Woolwich. Moxon, Stride and Whitelegg were all board members of the London, Tilbury and Southend Railway. Not to be outdone, the Eastern Counties Railway got in on the act – Rathbone was chairman, and Waddington deputy chairman respectively. The curiously named Hanameel Street is derived from the telegraphic address of a factory sited alongside it. The Winsor, of the terrace and park, was founder of the Gas, Light and Coke Company in Beckton. Pacific and Oriental Roads, Fisons Road, Tate Road and Lyle Park, need little further explanation; Factory Road, Dockland Street, Pier Road and Mill Road none whatsoever.

The names of the area, and the ideas and images they encapsulated, were projected into a wider sphere of significance through their use in the advertising of products and industries. 'Made in Silvertown' became an advertising slogan in its own right. West Ham's industrial achievement was marketed through its football club: West Ham United. Originally the works team of the Thames Ironworks, it adopted the crossed hammers as badge and nickname, as did the new Borough of West Ham in its civic crest, to signify the foundry, shipyards and engineering works from which they sprang.[22] Similar naming processes have continued into the twentieth century. As late as the 1960s, the then East Ham Council was naming North Woolwich's tower blocks after shipping lines associated with the Royal Docks: Dunedin, Queensland, Shaw, Brocklebank, Albion and Glen. But by the 1970s the high tide of industry was rapidly ebbing away and the 1980s and 1990s saw the appearance of a new post-industrial toponymy. Ironically, Will Thorne and Ben Tillett only got a look in once the jobs of the workers they organised had disappeared. Agnes, Fortis, Giralda, Satanita and Swale were the names of famous nineteenth century Thames sailing barges.[23] North Woolwich station was reborn as a museum; the cranes on Victoria Dock now only provide an attractive backdrop to the waterside apartments. A former grain silo in Silvertown got listed building status; English Heritage describes it as 'a statement of pure modernism'.[24] But the area no longer seems to be looking forward, now its toponymy is commemorative, dockland becomes 'Docklands': the same space but a different *place*.

The way that the naming process of particular streets and districts contribute to the construction of place is apparent. In comparing and contrasting the toponymic derivations of areas and streets in the north and south of the borough it is demonstrable that they do differ in some key aspects. This is most obvious in their functionality, broadly delineating the residential from the industrial. This underlies more subtle social divisions: between the artisan and the casual labourer, the clerk and the docker. As John Gorman again recalls:

Our street was a cut above Angel Lane, Bridge Road and the turnings around Stratford Market – well my mother thought so. The houses in St James Road had been built for mechanics during the industrialisation of the area during the 1870s and were in a reasonable state of repair ...

Other streets, even those in nearby turnings, were considered less salubrious. We certainly regarded the south of the borough, Custom House, Canning Town and Silvertown, as rougher areas, with their large population of casual dockers, gasworks labourers and factory workers in the chemical, sugar and rubber trades.[25]

Toponymic shift: processes and patterns

While the railway provided the social and economic foundation on which the new suburbs of the north were constructed, as the docks and other industries did in the south, the names added a further layer of values, images and meanings to the physical landscape. It is also apparent that once these geo-social entities emerged, the transport system had a large part to play in deciding which of them would predominate. In terms of both the original naming of individual neighbourhoods and suburbs, and subsequent toponymic shift, a link between place name and the transport system is evident. Returning once more to the property pages of the Newham Recorder (see Appendix 1), it is noticeable that virtually all the place names employed to describe the location of properties are also the names of rail or underground stations, unless they apply to one of the particularly upmarket areas such as the Woodgrange, Burges or Central Park Estates, or various parts of Beckton over a large area.[26] Upton and Plashet, just like Hallsville and Tidal Basin are no longer utilised in the social and spatial frameworks.

Whilst this is not the only process at work, there is little doubt that the presence of a station does tend to anchor an idea of place in the popular consciousness. Industries site themselves in relation to the transport network and their workers follow suit. Shops and other services cluster around them to catch the trade of the passing transport user. Stations become the social and economic focal point of the locality, and in doing so their names start to colonise the spaces from which they draw their trade – their hinterland. Other transport provision such as trams and buses also gravitate towards these hubs as part of an integrated system. In a historical context it is worth noting that even as early as 1913 a map and list of West Ham's tram lines made no reference whatsoever to Upton.[27] And modern London Transport bus maps follow the same pattern. Plashet, Upton, Hallsville and Tidal Basin are no longer shown. They have lost their meaning. They no longer exist.

As the city begins to be imagined in terms of its transport system, a process that inevitably grows as its use increases and becomes a means of mass communication, so the names of individual stations take on more prominence in the popular consciousness. It is no surprise that the London Underground system, 'The Tube', has developed into the unofficial motif or logo of the metropolis itself and the familiar red buses a widely recognised image. Now they encapsulate and propel the essence of the city into the wider consciousness as much as St Paul's Cathedral, Big Ben or Tower Bridge. The tube map's linear layout, and the overground railway network's depiction employing the same basic format, with stations existing in a subterranean virtuality only through their relation to each other, anonymises that which it excludes. It is easy to see how entities and geographies disincoporated by this imaging are similarly robbed of meaning and prominence in the public mind. We can easily imagine how, on a day to day basis, this would effectively marginalise and eradicate toponyms lacking this higher social and economic significance and solidity.

The explanatory 'Plashet, which is near Upton Park' shifted to the shorter description 'near Upton Park' and eventually over time to just 'Upton Park'. Perhaps in an isolated and static community such a process would not be as marked. But in an area as generally socially heterogeneous, and with a population as transient as Newham's this phenomenon would be significantly magnified. And as the administrative superstructure, and media and commercial discourses followed suit in creating and consolidating change these trends would be almost inevitable.

In the case of Upton Park it is also likely that the existence of West Ham United's football ground nearby has anchored the place in the popular consciousness; it is now a place of national, if not international, significance. Paradoxically Upton Park has never been the name of the stadium, its official title is 'The Boleyn Ground'. The station and suburb predate it by at least thirty years but through constant use it has come to colonise this space, eventually becoming fused in the popular imagination in one image.

What is striking, looking over the longer term, is the speed and extent to which new appellations were accepted and incorporated within the dominant discourses of the time. In many ways they are evidence of the sheer pace and dynamism of this manifestation of modernity; in a few decades replacing and re-ordering geographies that had been centuries in the making. It is hardly surprising that the old elite would mourn their passing. The names symbolically represented and gave meaning to their world, and when they changed so did the society that they had embodied. As Katherine Fry laments in the 1880s:

The green pastures and smiling fields, which skirted the various roadsides, the shady walks and pleasant country lanes have gradually disappeared. No longer do the rich and noble turn to the east, and instead of handsome mansions once inhabited by them, tall chimneys and busy factories, modern shops and inns, and dwellings of all shapes and sizes for the accommodation of Greater London meet the eye in every direction.[28]

Or as John Gorman seems to respond in recalling his 1930's childhood:

Lawyers, bankers and landlords were as rare as eleven bob notes in Stratford Market.[29]

Conclusion

The way that language represents objects, events, and relationships provides a uniquely powerful economy of reference. It offers a means for generating an essentially infinite variety of novel representations, and an unprecedented inferential engine for predicting events, organising memories, and planning behaviours. It entirely shapes our thinking and the ways we know the physical world.[30]

Names are the language of place, without them there is no *there*. That they both reflect and inform the cultural discourses operating in, upon, and from an individual locality, neighbourhood or community is evident. They speak from, speak for, and speak to, the wider world that they and their users order and inhabit. These constructions, taking the raw social and economic materials of their locale, define it, order it and give it meaning. The process is reciprocal: people make the names, the names contribute to the moulding of the cultural landscape, which in turn makes the people who make the names. They are, in and of themselves, cultural artefacts. That we live within their boundaries now is testament to their influence in making the present. They form part of our total lived environment; they articulate a lived and living past – literally a Public History.

Appendix

Breakdown of all place names/postcodes applied to properties in estate agents' advertisements in the *NewhamRecorder*, 12 May 1999.

Area descriptor used	Number of times used
Beckton	4
Beckton E6	3
Beckton E16	1
Mid-Beckton E6	1
North Beckton E6	1
North Beckton E16	1
Mid Beckton E6	1
West Beckton E16	2
Canning Town	6
Canning Town E16	4
Custom House	3
Custom House E16	3
East Ham	16
East Ham E6	21
East Ham South E6	1
Forest Gate	14
Forest Gate E7	17
Forest Gate E12	1
North Woolwich	1
Plaistow	13
Plaistow E13	19
Silvertown	1
Stratford	7
Stratford E15	7
Upton Park	3
Upton Park E13	1
West Ham	1
E6	3
E7	3
E12	1
E13	3
E15	1
Burges Estate	6
Central Park Estate	7
Woodgrange Area	1
High Street South Area	1
Off Green Street	2
Off Prince Regent's	1
Byron Ave	1
Cotswold Gardens	1

Notes

1. The London Borough of Newham was formed in 1965 from the amalgamation of the old County Boroughs of East and West Ham.
2. Francois Dossé, *New History in France: The Triumph of the Annales*, University of Illinois Press, Chicago, 1994, p. 178.
3. Marc Bloch, *The Historian's Craft*, Manchester University Press, Manchester, 1954, p. 33.
4. Dr Pagenstecher, *History of East and West Ham*, Wilson and Whitworth, Stratford, 1909, p. 201.
5. Katherine Fry, *History of Parishes of East and West Ham*, London 1888, printed for private circulation, p. 279. Katherine Fry was a member of the wealthy Quaker family. She was the daughter of the philanthropist and prison reformer Elizabeth Fry and resided for most of her life in Plashet House, on the site of modern day Plashet Park.
6. John Gorman, *Knocking Down Ginger*, Caliban Books, London, 1995, p. 8. Gorman is best known as a labour historian and grew up in Stratford in the 1930s and 1940s.
7. Roy Porter, *London: A Social History*, Penguin Books, London, 1996, p. 234.
8. John Gorman, 'Another East End: A Remembrance' in Geoffrey Alderman and Colin Holmes (eds.) *Outsiders and Outcasts – Essays in Honour of William J Fishman*, Duckworth, London, 1993, p. 177.
9. 'Life Story of Henry Jaques' (Manuscript c.1901) in Colin Pooley and Jean Turnbull, 'Changing Home and Workplace in Victorian London: the life of Henry Jaques, shirtmaker', *Urban History* 24 August 1997, pp. 170–171.
10. The Park, formerly the garden of Ham Park House, was opened to the public in 1874. It was part donated by the Gurney family, another branch of the local merchant/financier 'Quakerocracy', with the rest of the land purchase price contributed by the Corporation of the City of London and public donation. Although in Newham it is still maintained by the City Corporation.
11. HJ Dyos, 'Some reflections on the quality of urban life' in David Cannadine and David Reader, *Exploring The Urban Past – Essays in Urban History by HJ Dyos*, Cambridge University Press, Cambridge, 1982, p. 60.
12. West Ham Council Works Department Committee Minutes 12 January 1899.
13. Arthur Crouch, *Silvertown and Neighbourhood (Including East and West Ham), A Retrospect*, Thomas Burleigh, London, 1900, p. 7.
14. Ibid, p. 75.
15. James Thorne, *Handbook to the Environs of London* (1876), quoted in Donald Olsen, *The Growth of Victorian London*, Batsford, London, 1976, p. 273.
16. 'The Builder', Volume LI (1886), p. 656, in Olsen, *The Growth of Victorian London*, p. 273.
17. Ironically East and West Ham, which lay outside the metropolitan area, were denied access to the new sewer even though it ran right across the two boroughs. This led to severe sanitary and health problems, particularly in the marshy and poorly drained southern districts who were served by open sewers, cess pools and drainage ditches until the end of the nineteenth century.
18. James Thorne, *Handbook to the Environs of London* (1876) pp. 471–472, quoted in Olsen, *The Growth of Victorian London*, p. 272.
19. Colin Pooley and Jean Turnbull, 'Changing Home and Workplace in Victorian London', *Urban History*, Volume 24, August 1997, p. 149.
20. Dr Pagenstecher, *History of East and West Ham*, p. 196.
21. The Tidal Basin that gave its name to the surrounding area was a tidal lock that

enabled ships to enter and leave the docks. It had its own station on the North Woolwich line, until it was closed due to war damage in 1943, as did Custom House. The latter is still in use today.

22 West Ham United's other nickname is 'The Irons'. West Ham was incorporated as a County Borough in 1886. As well as the hammers, its coat of arms also included a ship to connote the importance of the docks. Those of East Ham, now adopted by Newham Council, also include the ship along with three torches, in reference to the gasworks. Beckton sewage works, the other major industry, receives less obvious recognition.

23 See Newham Council, Environmental Services Committee Minutes of 21 September 1982, Enclosure Y.

24 *Newham Recorder*, 21 April 1999.

25 John Gorman, *Knocking Down Ginger*, p. 9. As a digression it is worth contrasting Gorman's use of the word 'salubrious', here denoting a concept of class and respectability, with the context of its use by Henry Jaques, a hundred years or so before, where it is closely tied in with the idea of health and clean air. One can see that as healthy and respectable areas were linked in the same discourse, becoming one and the same thing. The concepts were elided into one another. This has resulted in the exact connotation and meaning of the word being subtly modified.

26 Obviously estate agents apply their own values and prejudices in describing the location of particular property and these should be read in this context. That having been said, these appellations are generally reflective of the popular discourse and the broad delineations are also used by other agencies and organisations.

27 *West Ham Corporation Tramways and Connections*, West Ham, West Ham Corporation, 1913.

28 Fry, *History of the Parishes of East and West Ham*, p. 279.

29 Gorman, *Knocking Down Ginger*, p. 9.

30 Terence Deacon, *The Symbolic Species: The Co-Evolution of Language and the Human Brain*, Penguin, London, 1998, p. 22.

'But it's not all nostalgia': Public History and local identity in Birmingham

Paul Long

Introduction: 'Us' and 'Them'

In *our* street, as in many others, there is an abundance of 'culture', 'history' and 'identity'. The stories told by a handful of families in our small row of Edwardian houses all end in Birmingham. Some begin here while others are traced in journeys from the West of Ireland, Serbia and Singapore. Mr P, who runs the shop across the street, comes from India. He sells the local newspaper, the *Evening Mail*, where one can read an opinion column concerning all matters parochial written by an egregious Australian called Ed Doolan. All of us, apart from my partner – who is from Hull – think of ourselves as Brummies. The question is: does 'Birmingham' think of 'Us' in the same way?

I am concerned here with questions of communal identity and representation in relation to an extraordinary proliferation in recent years of the writing and exhibiting of local history. The kind of history described is very much a public and popular one, relating the stories that Birmingham tells to the world and to itself. I ask what is invested – financially and culturally – and what is at stake when the city is imagined in particular ways. Where does authorship lie and what motives are discernable? Consequently, the individual perspective I have introduced is no vain conceit. Issues about the value and recording of the variety of 'our' stories, as those of ordinary people, are of paramount importance.

The notion of public history is useful in apprehending the aesthetic, aims, circulation and appeal of a range of local productions. These involve popular journalism, a cottage industry of publications, videos, walking guides and even music and variety performances. Such histories are usually conceived in biographical terms, where self and city are intimately linked. Although not exclusive, what characterises this work is that it concentrates roughly on the first half of the century. My aim is to explore the implicit disavowals of this focus, how ideas of community and history are managed in this way. I qualify this with reference to an 'official' site of history and culture, namely the Birmingham Museum and Art Gallery. The material dealt with here can be found in various guises across the country, usually dismissed in pejorative terms as 'heritage' and 'nostalgia'. One is wary of conflating local identities with Britishness or Englishness (there *are* differences), but tensions in the relationship of national and local are a vital aspect of the stories explored here.

'Something Direful in the Sound': narratives of loss, change and rejuvenation

In order to situate this study it is necessary to rehearse a narrative familiar to many in the city. Once a major industrial centre, Birmingham has experienced significant social and physical changes as a consequence of the economic turbulence of the 1970s. Founded upon an extensive manufacturing base, the 'City of a Thousand Trades' was unable to maintain export levels and between 1971 and 1976 alone upwards of 50,000 jobs were lost. This decline impacted heavily on the inner city, as many of the industries found there, reliant upon semi- or unskilled labour, closed or relocated. Inevitably this process exacerbated housing, environmental and intractable social problems. General disillusionment, urban unrest and decay met with ongoing turmoil in surviving industries, famously symbolised by British Leyland and the media's favourite shop steward 'Red Robbo'. Its citizens encumbered with *that* accent, Birmingham was perceived as a cultural wasteland, whose identifying icon was the execrable television soap opera Crossroads . If it was not the *sound* of us, it was the very name of the city that invited insult and injury. The shoddiness implied in the label 'Brummagem made' always tempered civic pride. As early as 1816 Jane

Austen wrote that this was not a place to promise much: 'One has no great hopes from Birmingham. I always say there is something direful in the sound'.[1] And in an age of decline the brute yet prodigious industry that facilitated the city's might and very existence no longer sustains its self-esteem.

In another context, Kevin Robins has dealt with some of the implications of such a situation, arguing that a communal acknowledgement of social change implies a capacity to relinquish aspects of a given identity.[2] But it is possible that tensions are likely to manifest themselves within the 'collective' when confronted with this possibility. The threat is of a 'loss' of something essential, aspects of identity felt to be materially valuable, qualities that make us what we are. In terms of *national* identity this essence might be located in the 'stiff-upper lip', the 'Dunkirk spirit' or a sense of 'fair play'. It is suggested that the threat conveyed by such change is met with *resistance*. For Robins, assertions of identity on behalf of 'the collective' set about elaborating myths and symbolic representations concerned with 'perennial meaning' and 'imaginary immortality' in the culture.[3]

This condition appositely describes some aspects of a modern, post-fordist Britain. Symptoms of anxiety are visible in the burgeoning heritage industry, in responses to globalisation, in our relationship with Europe and the threatened loss of the pound, seen as an index of sovereignty, cultural and historical integrity. Such threats are met by invocations of ossified history and the mythos and iconography of past glories are enlisted in order to alleviate national fears. The effects are at work even in current disputes over food. As one correspondent to the *Evening Mail* wrote: 'I'm not the only Briton who would love to give the French a symbolic gesture ...Winston Churchill's victory salute, or a variation of it springs to mind.'[4] This reliance upon greatness past only underlines the nature of its loss; it serves to distort contemporary dynamics and the actuality of change. In the same vein, who could forget John Major's disingenuous and partial mobilisation of 'Britishness' when resisting the imagined encroachments of European ideas (Federalism, Socialism, decent wages). In his Mansion House speech of April 1993 he cited George Orwell's wartime evocation of old maids bicycling to Holy Communion, the country of long shadows in county cricket grounds and warm beer. We were reassured that, come what may, 'Britain will survive unamendable in all essentials'.[5]

Not all citizens know this curiously Anglicised Britain or could imagine themselves as part of it. I know this place nonetheless, recognising exactly what John Major means, but like the Brixton boy, it is not a place he or I have ever lived in, could have, or are likely to. If one allies this vision with notions of 'middle-England', beloved of the media and current Labour administration, we can see how national identity has been remarkably exclusive in its definition. Tim Hall, for instance, has suggested that its references are associated with ideas of the South. Characteristics peculiar to the Home Counties have served to enclose 'the genteel, picturesque, the "cultural" and the rural';[6] Standard English and Received Pronunciation, have attained normative status. The disclosure of *un*Englishness – dialect and accented speech, the industrial regime, the bleak functionality *and* carnival of working class life for instance – has become associated with the North, creating it as marginal Other within the national space.

Exactly how 'Northern' or 'Southern' Birmingham might be is open to question, but it has been suggested that in terms of geography and representation it is in-between. Doubly marginalised the city has had to compete with the expectations involved in these polar reference points in order 'to assert an identity of its own making'.[7] In response, one way of viewing the attempted re-scripting of its physical spaces and identity is in the way it looks beyond the limitations of the national. For Hall the city imagines its future in terms of international 'high culture', manifested in prestige building projects such as the International Convention Centre and Symphony Hall. The D'Oyly Carte opera company was attracted here temporarily, while Sadlers Wells Ballet has shown more signs of staying by changing its name to the Birmingham Royal Ballet. Sculptures have been installed in public places: Raymond Mason's heroic Forward, Anthony Gormley's Tin Man and Dhruva Mistry's The River in Victoria Square. The latter features a female figure amidst fountain and waterfall whose high ideals are deflated by its colloquial label the 'Floozy in the Jacuzzi'. There has also been a pedestrianisation of shopping areas and talk of boulevards lined with cafes and trattoria. Consequently, the city presents its spaces as spectacular theatrical experiences, affecting a continental élan, challenging its unsophisticated image and (dis)placement in the national imaginary.

The impetus for this change was of course predicated on an understanding and *acceptance* of the city's history as peripheral, part of those myths of Northern decline and post-industrialisation. Inevitably then the maintenance of this image involves the marginalisation of perspectives, characteristics and cultural practices felt to be unsavoury or unsellable. Hall has argued that the idea of the 'City of a Thousand Trades' as a place of smokestacks, slums, those Northern imageries, are exactly what the 'City' has had to refute or alter through the process of urban regeneration and redefinition. Paradoxically then, for a city renowned as the hub of the industrial world, 'reconstruction' involves a problematisation of a coherent past predicated on generally unfashionable images of mechanisation, mass production and labour. What *is* available therefore are selective and 'polished' versions of the past appropriate to 'the entire tourist attraction that Birmingham has become'.[8]

Once left to rot in the years of decline, the Jewellery Quarter has become a key site in this transformation of Birmingham 'into a world class city'. A central feature is the Smith and Pepper premises in Vyse Street: the 'factory that time forgot'.[9] This is preserved as it was for 80 years until its workshops closed in 1981. The theatrical presentation of this space was realised in prosaic manner when the Museum of the Jewellery Quarter commissioned specialist company Pattern 23 Theatre to produce a dramatised version of the life of this area during the last century. Gwen Williams' *Around the Clock* used theatre, music and the Smith and Pepper building 'to evoke the distant voices and working lives of the people'.[10] The area now appears in Morrisonian guise as a centre for arts and crafts. It celebrates the artisanal, individuality and creativity; the unattractive alienating experience of rationalised mass production is of course unacknowledged. A measure of the success of the place is the publicity for its cleanliness, safety and the impressive series of bars and restaurants ready to cater to tourist needs. Indeed one advertising feature notes that few of the thousands who visit the area each year would imagine that it was once 'so dirty, ill-lit and dilapidated'.[11]

Nearby, Gas Street Basin's redbrick factories, warehouses and stinking, polluted canals have also been reclaimed. Its bars, clubs and restaurants are a central feature of the Broad Street development. Visiting this place on a Friday or Saturday night in particular one might be forgiven for thinking that the locals are involved in a non-stop party. Yet in terms of the money spent on *this* city, one wonders whose benefit all of it is for? In 1998 the G8 Summit, the Lions Club International AGM, and the Eurovision Song Contest accounted for many of the 2.24 million people from abroad who visited the region, filling the hotels, restaurants and bars and spending £668 million.[12] In Hall's analysis one has an impression of the ubiquitous 'City' represented by a coterie of businessmen, media and the Council itself, all involved in this reinscribing of local identity. It reveals no contradiction to suggest, however,, that within this space, within the Council itself for that matter, there are multiple imaginaries of Birmingham directly or indirectly competing with this powerful and successful cosmopolitan vision. As with Robins' description of reactions to change, Hall also uses a notion of *resistance*. Aspects of this can be found in the kind of local histories that speak directly to residents of the area. While such material might also be partial, presenting the past as spectacle and commodity, the accumulated effect is of the assertion of a Birmingham demonstrating a type of authenticity that is uncalled for in a tourist brochure.

'Dear Nostalgic...' the spectacle of local history[13]

Walking into the enormous Waterstone's bookshop on New Street in the centre of the city, one finds a local history section that dwarfs that devoted to national history. This is evidence of a significant industry that has flourished in the last twenty-five years or so, developing from amateur origins to become a highly professional and competitive field. Brewin Books, the largest regional publisher, offers over 150 titles, all in print. Its owner Alan Brewin recalls that when he began the only publications available were typewritten, stapled books, 'printed in the garden shed' and left on sale or return at W.H. Smith. Brewin's most popular series comprises nearly 30 books by Alton Douglas which have sold in excess of 300,000 copies. Typical titles are *Birmingham Shops*, *Birmingham at Work*, *Memories of Birmingham*.[14] Douglas was formerly a busy comic and actor who had appeared in Crossroads. In 1979 he was asked to host a new series produced by BBC Midlands called Know Your Place, an inter-town quiz for TV. Taking on the vacant role of scriptwriter as well as quizmaster, he discovered after several series that there was a gap in the book market. Few companies published local history books dealing with living memories, especially the Midlands' experience of the last war. So,in 1982, in conjunction with the *Evening Mail* he published *Birmingham at War Vol.1*, 'an immediate success'. Subsequent books expanded the historical range and type of coverage. Mainly pictorial, these collections are advertised as comprising: 'lots of ads, newspaper cuttings and posters. We cram as many items into each book as possible, at the same time we insist that they remain inexpensive to buy'.[15] They invite us to 'Turn Back the Page to Yesterday',[16] suggesting something qualitatively different to formal academic history: 'the emphasis throughout is on nostalgia.'

In much the same vein advertising for a series of books published by Birmingham Library Services promises 'Fond Memories'.[17] Twelve titles, each containing 200 photographs, trace the history of various neighbourhoods. Each has a sepia-toned front cover portraying groups of Victorians, Edwardians, scout meetings, and schoolchildren. The cover of *Old Harborne* by Roy Clarke[18] (also the cover of the brochure) shows a bare-chested, short-trousered boy running along a railway platform watched by other children and young women; older people are visible but are confined to the background. The dress places it about the late 1930s, and the impression is of youthful vitality, although this is qualified by the autumnal sepia-tones. The connotations of such unselfconsciousness are of innocence and authenticity.

Despite Douglas' success the project of local history finds its apotheosis in the work, and celebrity, of Dr. Carl Chinn. Chinn, 'the people's "professor" – the West Midlands favourite historian',[19] is Community Historian at the University of Birmingham, a post co-funded by the Council's Leisure Services Department. That his unbridled enthusiasm and approach to local history has struck a chord with Brummies is testified to by the longevity of a weekly two-page spread in the *Evening Mail* and a daily slot on local radio where he 'brings your memories to life of old Brummagem'. He has contributed to television programmes, released musical compact discs and videos, made regular public appearances to discuss his work and appeared in old-time variety shows alongside local entertainers. A tireless champion of the city and region, his project is avowedly biographical in motivation. His sense of self and identity is linked to the city and a particular notion of community. Recalling the bleak years of decline, he laments the lack of focus and direction evident in the city at that time. For him a spell of unemployment at the beginning of the 1980s led into higher education.[20] This move facilitated his writing and archival work and the development of an archive that already contains over 9000 letters and oral interviews. His aim is to reclaim a proud heritage, described by the working-classes of Birmingham, a profoundly political act in many ways, even though he has an 'apolitical' public persona. His negotiation between the role of academic and popular historian is very revealing.

Chinn's weekly spread in the Saturday edition of the *Evening Mail* is in its fifth year, bringing the past to life in quite precise ways. Eliciting a voluminous correspondence about readers' memories, he explores the histories and culture of trades and firms, pubs, cinemas and streets. There is an indefatigable mapping of the physical and personal geographies of the city, many of which have disappeared or are now unrecognisable. What we have is a remembrance and description of the ordinary. The written word is complemented with photographs familiar from Douglas' popular collections. Layer upon layer of names and anecdotes give a three dimensional texture to vanished scenes. In one contribution a correspondent describes Furnace Lane in the Lozells area, a cobblestoned alleyway about 10 feet wide which started near the corner of Gower Street and Guildford Street and ran south-east for about half a mile, crossing Gerrard Street, then going up the hill, crossing Clifford Street and finally ending at its junction with Porchester Street.[21] This is a psychic space one could walk through, so to speak. Such material resonates with descriptions and the very sounds of the streets; the calls of traders, mothers and children ring out. Similarly, the note that 'every part of Brummagem...had its smells',[22] elicits an olfactory visit to the past. Readers recall gasworks, the damp odour of the railways of the steam and coal age, breweries and the spicy tang of sauce factories such as Holbrook's and H.P.

The tone of these weekly pieces is distilled in a series of songs written with local musician Laurie Hornsby. These are collected on two compact discs The Brummagem Air and Any Road Up!, which evoke the kind of sing-along one could expect at any of Chinn's public performances. Set to barrel-organ, alehouse piano and banjo (the obvious reference point is the work of East End duo Chas 'n' Dave), the tunes seek to 'recapture the spirit of bygone days'. The cumulative effect of lyric and arrangement is a bypassing of the popular music of the past forty, if not one hundred years, to something felt to be warmer, more authentically and organically popular. We return to the days of anodyne courtships, woodbines and demob suits in Underneath the Snow Hill Clock. Accompanied by a whirling organ we run through a role call of the many disappeared movie houses in Let's Go to the Pictures. For a 'dollar' we take a bus ride around the many neighbourhoods, Heaven on the Number 11, and recall local breweries on the pub crawl to end all pub crawls in A Nice Drop of Ale. Chinn addresses 'people like us', conveying a sense of identification, historical continuity and solidarity. 'People like us' are those who did inhabit this milieu – as adults or as children. Perhaps by virtue of age, the inarguable benefits of the Welfare State and other transformations that have divorced us from that world so completely, we are all now outsiders visiting this world vicariously. Such spaces, and those described in sepia-tinted and black and white photos, through evocations and testimonies of hardship, have been (re-) presented in similar ways before, beginning with the visitation of darkest England by adventurous middle-class social reformers of the nineteenth century such as Henry Mayhew. The trend was developed by George Orwell in *The Road to Wigan Pier* and J.B. Priestley in *English Journey*.

In the post-war era authors such as Richard Hoggart added a new inflection to this project. Born into this milieu, but escaping through education, they returned to pay tribute to the cultures and values that had nurtured them – even as these were disappearing or in the process of change. Hoggart's *The Uses of Literacy*, published in 1957,[23] had a remarkable impact on the way in which people thought of class and culture in British society (alongside the work of Raymond Williams it effectively inaugurated the field of cultural studies). It offered a sensitive and sympathetic portrayal of a world, experiences and voices then still rarely acknowledged in the public sphere. Hoggart's influence has been noted in the cinematic adaptations of contemporaneous working-class novels and plays such as *Saturday Night, Sunday Morning* and *A Taste of Honey*, as well as resonating in the early development of television's Coronation Street.[24] Despite a realist guise, these texts present the slum as spectacle, subject to a particular poetic inflection. The suspicion here is that one is still privy to an outsider's vision – whether that of a middle-class director or returning scholarship boys like Hoggart or Tony Warren (the creator of Coronation Street). Chinn himself has paid tribute to Hoggart's work[25] and the typical figures found in *The Uses of Literacy* resonate in reader's letters. One correspondent, for instance, wrote of his mother as 'the salt of the earth, bringing us up clean and tidy and to respect our elders'.[26] This perspective offers a way of understanding our material as a form of resistance, a reaction to changes in the city. What values and ideas are present in this older, class-bound version of Birmingham and what does it have to say about current developments?

Remembering and forgetting: 1
The idea that this mode of history can be conceived as an antidote to the current 'high culture' approach by the city is a stimulating one. It presents a version of a Birmingham lost not just to inexorable time but to the bulldozer and surveyor and suggests the evocation of a place that 'was taken away when they cleared up after the bombs'[27] or 'swept away by the forming of the Inner Ring Road'.[28] One wonders to what extent the vision and impersonality of contemporary projects is perceived to be of a piece with such a process, and current redevelopment has indeed had to work against this notorious phase in the city's history.

Plans for redevelopment in fact began before 1939. The present situation has parallels in the proposals made at that time for major structural changes, constituting a visionary attempt to situate the city at the forefront of the twentieth century. Figures such as Chief Engineer and Surveyor Herbert Manzoni saw themselves as following in the footsteps of arch modernists such as Le Corbusier and Walter Gropius. The impulse was genuinely progressive in a wider sense, aiming to improve the lot of all citizens, especially those condemned to live in cramped and dirty housing. Slum clearances, general repair and redevelopment took place over three decades but were carried out with most energy in the 1960s. Monuments such as the high-rise tower blocks and estates of Castle Bromwich and Chelmsley Wood, the Bull Ring, 'Spaghetti

Junction', and the Central Library testify to that moment and the ambivalent feelings with which it is regarded. The results were not widely appreciated at the time nor has history been kind; Prince Charles famously derided the library for looking like a place where books are burnt rather than stored.

Ever since the 1960s there has been a prevailing sense of disillusionment with that period. City architect Nicola Cox has suggested that: 'the strength of feeling of Birmingham's people, which gave way to nostalgia, came from the profound sense of loss felt at the demolition of familiar and much loved buildings, and the seeming lack of control over developments which affected them.'[29] Reactions to the era are exemplified by the Black Country Society, a organisation outside the city whose aim is to foster general interest in the region, past present and future. The Society was established in 1967 'as a reaction to the "bigger-the-better" policies being pursued in the late 1950s and 1960s over a wide-field: local government, industry, commerce, education, and health. In connection with some of these it meant that our heritage was being swept away in the process.'[30]

I would suggest that the environment that was created in Birmingham, primarily based upon the needs of the motor car, was felt to be extremely impersonal and alienating. Post-war housing design for instance has been described as resulting in standardised buildings with little vernacular reference.[31] While the same might be said of the original slums and back-to-backs they replaced, at least over time the residents of the older housing had developed some kind of relationship with blue brick, mortar and cobbles. Cultural identities and structures grew up, and for better or worse were inextricable from those places. In an aesthetic sense the city of the 1960s was intended to produce the shock of the new. In contrast, even slums had a warm glow of familiarity. Thus the city's slum quarters are now fetishised and mentioned in the same breath as more imposing features such as the old library or Market Hall. The modern Birmingham has aged, of course it has, but it has never invited affection or the accretion of 'historicalness' in the same way that our classical buildings do.

Although he has written about the entire range of Birmingham's history and is a champion of its present and future, Carl Chinn concentrates primarily on the period before the 1960s. This coincides with his academic interests and his conviction, as for many of his audience, that a 'whole way of life' was disrupted and swept away when modernisers moved in. Something seemingly organic about inner-city communities such as Digbeth, Hockley, Aston or Small Heath was extinguished arbitrarily from *without*. Chinn's main concern has been with the working class at the more precarious end of the economic scale, those existing between bouts of abject poverty in unemployment and relative prosperity in semi-skilled work. Crucially then, this was not merely a way of life 'lost' to us but one that was not afforded a great deal of attention in the first place. It is here that one finds values and an identity worthy of celebration and investigation, exactly that elided by ongoing redevelopment.

On one level the history of Douglas, Chinn and others, provides a recreation of that curiously industrial yet pre-modern version of the city. Recounting the names of streets, pubs, schools and shops, attended by a cast of long gone folk invites one into the texture and values of the past. The effect of Chinn's accomplished work, in all its variety, is to define the past as a place of community. And community is by implication the property of the working classes who inhabited this milieu, 'hard-working and neighbourly folk' who gave areas 'a strong sense of identity'.[32] The work is addressed directly to a constituency that recognises this discourse and the very experience of labour, community and often hardship. This is explicit in songs such as 'Any Road Up!':

> Any road up we'll have a little sup, tonight
> Wash out the swarf and then take off, tonight
> It might be a birthday or wet the babby's 'ead*
> Strike me pink, if you can't have a drink you might as well be dead
> ...have a strip down, swill, and we'll feel alright.

(*the pronunciation is important)

Added to an extensive historical texturing in Chinn's work are descriptions of the dignity of labour and dignified poverty, an ethos of making-do, the kinds of rituals and culture attendant upon proud and sometimes desperate lives eked out amidst the geography of the slums. It is a world of back-to-backs, shared toilets, betting and cheap Bank Holiday excursions. The spoken introduction to the song 'You're OK' advises, 'It don't matter if you've only got a newspaper for the tablecloth

... a peg rug on the floor. It don't even matter if you've only got distemper on the walls.' 'You' *are* OK because of the recognition that life is about 'carin', sharin' and grinnin' and bearin''.

This approach inscribes the ordinary and the everyday in the city's historical space. I would suggest that such a project is at one with wider trends that have been developing since 1945.There has been a new-found respect for working-class cultures, dialects and rituals, the encouragement of people's stories, while 'history from below' has paid attention to a wholly neglected area of the national narrative. If the success of small publishers producing local histories in the last twenty years may look like a consequence of Thatcherism, their practices owe much to the tiny radical, community presses and projects that grew up in the 1960s and 1970s. Here I am thinking of Queenspark in Brighton and Centerprise in London, which presented the writing and stories of ordinary people in books such as *Working Lives: a people's autobiography of Hackney*. Chinn's work had forerunners such as the The Tindal Street Memory Group whose aim was one of 'writing it down before its all gone'.[33]

This kind of work is very much a communal, democratic concern testifying to a vocal humanity that, by design or accident, has been disregarded to some extent by present developments and trends in Birmingham. Perhaps it is all that can be done to give name to those who were hitherto nameless in historical narratives, but even in the enlisting of such an unfashionable concept as class as an abiding category Chinn's work worries at a cosmopolitan identity. He assumes no distance or authoritative voice in order to qualify his own status as organiser of this material and as qualified historical 'expert'. He has made a virtue of the vernacular. The broad Brummie accent he speaks with and maintains in his role as radio and TV presenter adds weight to the popular and democratic appeal of his work. This deference to some extent allows for a sense of the value of the ordinary voice. At times he seeks to present the written word in the demotic style of his ideal respondents and audience. 'Her mom had always told her, "As y'mek y're bed y'lie on it", but my oath she'd never med this bed and often she roared deep within herself "My God, what ave I done to ave such an ard life!"[34] He has sought to legitimate local accent and dialect words, locating them in the work of 'our Warwickshire lad William Shakespeare'.[35] The language and region are closely linked, things that change and should welcome new trends:

> But what we should also not do is abandon our old words just for the sake of fashion or modernity. We should use our dialect terms, nurture them and pass them on to our children's children as they were passed on so preciously to us.[36]

Remembering and forgetting: 2

As I have suggested, many of the photographs of slum life seen in contemporary local histories present as spectacle those truths once confronted by the social investigators of the last century. Seebohm Rowntree, who produced a number of studies of poverty, said of his journeys into working class districts that that 'the pinched faces of the ragged children told their own tale of poverty and privation'.[37] This transparency might have been obvious to middle-class outsiders, but people went to great lengths to maintain the privacy that afforded respectability. To seek charitable aid at times of desperation meant surrendering to the interrogation of outsiders and the advertising of one's failure. As David Vincent has said, 'Families became poor when they could no longer keep their stories private.'[38]

That once guarded stories, exceptional and everyday are increasingly entering the public domain is an indication of significant changes in people's lives and the distance gained from such times. In this respect, one can identify what one might term a genre of hardship to describe such narratives. A local template is provided by Kathleen Dayus' celebrated series beginning with *Her People* (1982), and continuing with *Where There's Life* (1985), *All My Days* (1988) and *Best of Times* (1991). Such tales, difficult to tell, sometimes confrontational or confessional, detail often horrendous conditions and events tempered by moments of relief called 'good times'. A.A. Hasker's self-published *Cows Didn't Graze in Brum* offers a chance to take a trip to the 'dark days during the great depression'. An advertisement for the book makes a virtue of its authenticity, it pulls no punches in its depictions of slum scenes and suffering:

> A nostalgic trip for those survivors of that era. A glimpse into the past for the younger generation. The sadness of witnessing the tragic death of a

young mother, "The Back Street Abortionist". Back breaking work in an ill lit and filthy factory that clung tenaciously to the Dickensian era for starvation wages and long hours. Moonlight flits from the rent dodgers. It's all there vividly told.[39]

Local publisher John Roberts of Quercus Books complains of the tendency towards nostalgia in most memoirs and has added Helen Butcher's *The Treacle Stick* to his list. The 82-year-old author recalls 'growing up in harsh times with ... a cruel, demanding mother'.[40] From the same imprint and in a similar vein is *Us Kids* by Carole Anne Stafford and Alan Crowe. This deals with life in 1940s Ladywood, amidst damp, cockroach infested houses, where boozing provided an escape and also exacerbated personal tensions. 'But in these rough and ready families there was also closeness, perseverance, humour, real affection and perhaps a little hope.'[41]

The presentation of 'life's rich tapestry' in such stories means that they are not necessarily at odds with the field of nostalgia and are certainly at one with the exploration and reclaiming of a grittily authentic Birmingham. That said, notions of celebration and identification in stories of this nature always involve personal and public anxieties about their disclosure. This idea can be illustrated with reference to an uncle of mine who produced a novel based on a life spent as a professional criminal. Those who are explicitly worried about their place in its disclosures have protested about this work. My aunt too decided to turn her memories into narrative, directly inspired by Dayus' books. Prepared for her grandchildren, typed up and bound by a friend, her work also delves into tendentious territory – in the familial and public sense. It presents a familiar tale of poverty and hardship, but in exploring the life of children born to a Bengali father and English mother it serves to highlight issues normally absent in the genre, notably that of race and racism. As she writes:

> I came home one day and said to Mom I was fighting with a friend Janet and her dad came out and said, "Hop it you little nigger." He said, "in the war they couldn't get the ships through with oranges and bananas, the ships got torpedoed and were sunk, but they managed to get you blacks over." "Sod 'em", Mom said, "Tek one of the babby's in the pram for a walk".[42]

Those areas associated with 'authentic' Birmingham devastated by bombs or unsympathetic developers in Chinn's narrative have become the 'inner-city' and the term and geographical area are now inextricably associated with migrant communities – linking the threat and actuality of change and loss with Otherness – those identifiably from *without*. It was in Birmingham, in April 1968, that Enoch Powell famously signalled his reaction to this threat. Like Virgil in the Aeneid he saw 'the River Tiber foaming with much blood' when faced with the prospect of change and the appearance of cultures that for him formed no part of History and could therefore mean only trouble. In such imaginaries the past is untroubled by the issue of race and by implication the problems that migrants bring with them and upon themselves. As one local memoir recalls:

We didn't see many foreigners in Birmingham during the 'twenties and 'thirties. Occasionally a Frenchman, wearing a beret, would come to the door, carrying a string of onions: very infrequently one would see a black man in the street, but even in London foreigners were not very numerous. As a consequence, xenophobia hardly existed, the strongest emotion of the Englishman towards visitors from overseas being that of mild curiosity. The British Empire spanned the earth and its beneficent role was, we were encouraged to believe, self-evident.[43]

Implicit reactions to threats of a cultural nature and their relationship with history are abiding concerns of the letters page of the *Evening Mail* newspaper. Culprits for the decline of the nation, the quality of 'Englishness', manners, gentility and morality[44] include liberals, do-gooders, and what I once saw referred to as 'the ethnics' (sic). And it is race, which again and again is the defining threat to identity, illuminating exclusive ideas of community and history. The *Evening Mail's* pronounced suspicion of multiculturalism in articles and leaders is underwritten by correspondents who explicitly question the spending of Council money on the celebration and perpetuation of other faiths and traditions. Every year there is a voluminous mailbag bemoaning the lack of regard for St George's Day while the Afro-Caribbean, Asian and indeed Irish communities seem to have festival days and traditions more worthy of respect and support. Unsurprisingly then, an abiding topic in the letters page is 'political correctness'. Whatever this concept might mean it has come to connote something pejorative and the *Evening Mail* itself has consistently represented it as something lunatic, anti-common-sense and consequently anti-English. And readers agree.

I am not being facetious in observing that an abiding suggestion is that Britain fought on the wrong side in the last war. Correspondents regularly give the impression that Englishness stands for values that are inimical to human rights in general. Egalitarianism – whether based on race, class, gender or sexuality – the democratic right to trial and the presumption of innocence until proven guilty, these are all antithetical to tradition. As Mrs B Browning of Northfield suggested: 'Political correctness is a scourge in our history and our democratic rights as a sensible, civilised nation. Increasingly we see everything we cherished and worked to achieve in our country being attacked and whittled away by the workshy, race relations industry and the zealots of political correctness.'[45] One of Chinn's respondents talking of the 'alternative English' of the 1920s and 1920s observed that 'It was all politically incorrect, but who cares?'[46] Another letter writer complains of the debilitating effect of this egalitarian project, that 'It is only a matter of time before the National Anthem and probably the Union Jack is scrapped in case it offends too many people.'[47] The question for many has become 'Are we living in Britain or aren't we?'[48]

'Not just white, not just male, not just adult, not just Cadbury's' – Public History and other voices

One might be affording the such views too much significance by implying that they reflect the opinion of the majority. The letters page of the *Evening Mail* is a forum that does occasionally allow for other viewpoints. These contest popular, monolithic and cosy views of history,[49] sometimes celebrating Birmingham's demographic developments and diversity. It is important to acknowledge that the city is a place where ideas about identity and history compete, are resisted or contested. On one hand there are those who protest the promotion of a multi-faith, multi-cultural Birmingham. On the other hand those who might be expected to benefit from such attention find that where migrant communities have been mentioned positively it is once again with an eye on tourism and consumption. Thus, there is talk of promoting the exotic cultures located in the 'Balti Belt', 'Chinese Quarter' and so on. There has even been mention of the development of a Sikh village on the Soho Road in Handsworth. Aware of this limiting view, a number of public exhibitions in recent years have begun to pay detailed attention to the experience of people of Asian, African, Caribbean and indeed Irish origin. *Being Here, Roots of the Future: Ethnic Diversity in the Making of Britain* and *Home from Home* have all made space for particular historical presences. They have dealt with the question of identity in highly original and subtle ways, conscious of the fact that these are stories generally unwritten, involved in a problematic relationship with the story that the city and indeed the nation tells itself.

Ivan Karp has written that the collections and activities one finds in museums are intimately bound to assertions about what counts as art, taste, heritage and science: 'Hence they are bound up with assertions about what is central or peripheral, valued or useless, known or marginal.'[50] Museums in this framework can be thought of as legitimating sites involved in the confirmation of tradition in times of change. Alternatively they might exhibit a form of leadership where change is positively acknowledged and negotiated, although not necessarily celebrated uncritically.

Situated next to the Birmingham Council House, the Corporation Art Gallery is now a Grade II listed building, purpose built in a neo-classical style in 1885 during the great municipal era of the city. It says everything about high-culture, Empire, acquisition and display even before one enters its imposing doorway. It was established as a site where artisans great and small of the 'City of a Thousand Trades' could compare and admire the products of other cultures. But in a post-industrial, post-colonial city, the original exhibits and the impetus behind them have become somewhat irrelevant, if not suspiciously patronising and colonialist. In recent years the Museum has attempted to address some of these concerns with some success. Initiatives such as Gallery 33 for instance, have re-framed 'exotic' collections, undermining and questioning the traditional manner of their exhibition and the guiding assumptions behind it.[51]

A new proposal with the unwieldy name of the Brumillennium Project seeks to do new things with local history. In fact, one suspects that it offers a direct response to the way in which the recent past and social changes have been treated, or not, by local industry. The main purpose of this project is the construction of a usable 'People's History'. Its elements will comprise the view of the city as seen by its citizens, a catalogue of millennial events, stories of older generations, but also an attempt to apprehend what has happened to the city and its inhabitants since 1945. 'It will contain the real voice of Birmingham's people and span the full range of personal, community and business life of our community.'[52] It is explicit about its inclusiveness that will be, in the words of director Brian Lantz, 'Not just white, not just male, not just adult, not just Cadbury's'.[53] Sizable resources are already available concerning the history of the Cadbury and Rover firms, both still considerable employers in Birmingham. But there is little material available on the smaller businesses that constituted Birmingham's reputation as the 'City of a Thousand Trades'. Likewise, community groups often dealing with local or single issues – such as protesting redevelopment – have come and gone without being recorded. It has been suggested too that members of the city's ethnic groups 'have been turned away so often that they have given up trying to tell their stories to "outsiders".' Of course, the project insists that it *does* want to listen to 'white adult males from Cadbury's too, but not *just* them.'[54]

A remarkable amount of technology has been deployed to research this work construct the displays. The aim is to make this event 'fun' which 'may be the key to unlocking stories that have yet to be told'. Given the reasons why stories have been concealed or excluded and the tensions involved one must wonder at the wisdom of this approach. Whether stories can be told and how they are received is always a concern. For instance, a comparable project is the BBC's massive oral history project The Century Speaks, which has striven to achieve something of this kind across the country. It is depressing to discover that its Midlands producer has received several racist letters following a programme that dealt specifically with the immigrant experience in the area.[55] Whatever results for the Museum, the project and new collecting policies are part of a long-term vision. The planning and completion of a new and prestigious Birmingham History Gallery will place such stories firmly in a public space and narrative.

Conclusions
From a global perspective it is impossible to see Birmingham's past as the engine room of modernity as unconnected with colonialism and empire. Nuts, bolts, pins, buttons, bicycles

and of course guns and men were sent on to distant places to which many of Birmingham's citizens can today trace some ancestry. Acknowledging issues to do with race or ethnicity and its association with constructions of Otherness does not constitute an attempt to speak on anyone else's behalf; that would be arrogant. Such observations come from an interest in the manner in which those who inhabit the socio-cultural margins in this country have changed in recent decades. After all, affording the lower classes respect, cultural and social attention, including them in the national imaginary is a relatively recent development. The exhaustive nature of Carl Chinn's project demonstrates this well enough.

What is important is that signalling awkward issues and telling difficult stories erodes the discrete boundaries of history culture, nation and locality, exposing the manner in which these things are represented to ourselves and to others. Carol Kammen of Cornell University, who writes a regular syndicated column for specialist magazines entitled 'On Doing Local History', has addressed some of these ideas. She describes how a conscious and unconscious self-censorship is sometimes involved in the writing of such histories. There is sensitivity to the perceived needs of the local community, 'because it provides tourist destinations ... because it provides good "copy" for publicity and interesting locales'. She suggests that this concentration elides processes of development and change, focusing instead on a few standard topics. For instance, there is neglect of the 'study of local crime, race relations and racial conflict, the actions of strikers and bosses, and political topics of all sorts. These are legitimate subjects to pursue but are generally about divisive moments in our past; they do not promote a picture of a unified community consciousness and of a harmonious past.'[56]

Explicit or not the kinds of histories dealt with in this essay all have something to say about what community is, where it lies and who belongs within its borders. Speaking to outsiders or between us, even the most innocuous of works says something about who we are, what we are and who we are not. This very public process is always shifting and open to contest, even as some insist upon the completeness and finality of culture, identity and the historical story.

Notes

1. Jane Austen, *Emma*, Oxford University Press, Oxford & New York, 1995, p. 280.
2. Kevin Robins, 'Interrupting identities: Turkey/Europe' in Stuart Hall and Paul du Gay (eds), *Questions of Cultural Identity*, Sage Publications, London, pp. 61-86.
3. Ibid. p 61.
4. Sally Hartley, 'Stand up for Britain' (Letter) in *Evening Mail*, 20.10.99, p. 6.
5. Quoted in Marina Warner, 'Home: Our Famous Island Race' in *Independent*, 3.03.94, p. 22.
6. Tim Hall, '(Re)Placing The City: Cultural relocation and the city as centre' in John Westwood and John Williams (eds), *Imagining Cities: scripts, signs, memory*, Routledge, London & New York, 1996, p. 209.
7. Ibid, p. 211.
8. David Whinyates, 'Jewel in the crown' in 'Modern Times: A look at the events that have shaped Birmingham today ... An Evening Mail Souvenir Special' in *Evening Mail*, 27.10.99, p 36.
9. Anon, 'Focus on the Jewellery Quarter' in 'Modern Times: A look at the events that have shaped Birmingham today ... An Evening Mail Souvenir Special' in *Evening Mail*,27.10.99, p. 36.
10. Birmingham City Council. Department of Leisure and Community Services. *What's on in Birmingham Museums and Art Gallery*, August–September 1999.
11. Whinyates, 'Jewel in the Crown', p. 34.
12. Anon, 'Tourists at the heart of it' in *Evening Mail*, 15.10.99, p. 12.
13. From an advert for Alton Douglas' books in *The Presenter*, Issue 1, Millennium Edition AD 2000. (Brewin Books publicity pamphlet), p. 3.
14. Alan Brewin, personal communication with the author. 2.11.1999.
15. Advertisement in *The Presenter*, Issue 1, Millennium Edition AD 2000, p. 2.
16. *The Presenter*, Issue 1, Millenium Edition AD 2000, p. 1.
17. (Advertising pamphlet) 'Fond Memories' produced by Birmingham City Council, Department of Leisure and Community Services.
18. Roy Clarke, *Old Harborne*, Alan Sutton, Bath, 1994.
19. Quoted on a BBC Radio WM portrait/autograph card sent out on request.
20. Carl Chinn, personal communication with the author 30.03.97 and 12.11.99.
21. Quoted in Carl Chinn, 'Lanes lost in the mists of time' in *Evening Mail*, 30.10.99, p. 18.
22. Carl Chinn. 'Just what the doctor ordered' in *Evening Mail*, 23.10.99, p. 18.
23. Richard Hoggart, *The Uses of Literacy: Aspects of working-class life with special reference to publications and entertainments*. Chatto &Windus, London, 1957.
24. See Andrew Higson, 'Space, Place, Spectacle: Landscape and Townscape in the 'Kitchen Sink', *Film*, pp. 133–156, and Terry Lovell, 'Landscapes and Stories in 1960s British Realism', pp. 157–177 in Andrew Higson (ed.) *Dissolving Views: Key Writing on British Cinema*, Cassell, London, 1996.
25. As discussed with Hoggart himself in Chinn's daily Radio WM show, 8.11.99.
26. Quoted in Carl Chinn. 'Picture captures crowning moment' in *Evening Mail*, 2.10.99, p. 18.
27. Mrs D Dyer in Carl Chinn. 'Lanes lost in the mists of time' in *Evening Mail*, 30.10.99. p. 19.
28. Carl Chinn, Ibid.
29. Birmingham City Council. Department of Planning and Architecture. *Shaping*

     the Seventies:1970s Architecture in Birmingham, Birmingham, 1998.
30. The Black Country Society's 1999 Summer Programme of Guided Walks, Kingswinford, page 4.
31. Nicola Coxon, *Signalling the Sixties: 1960s Architecture in Birmingham*, Birmingham City Council. Planning and Architecture Department, 1997.
32. Ibid.
33. See for instance Alan Mahar (ed), *Writing it Down Before It's All Gone: working class life in Balsall heath between the wars, local history from written memories of Tindal Memory Writing Group*. Tindal Association for School and Community and Art Link, 1984.
34. Carl Chinn, 'Getting all steamed up' in *Evening Mail*, 14.08.99, p. 18.
35. Carl Chinn, 'The stuff of legends!' in *Evening Mail*, 7.08.99, p.18.
36. Ibid.
37. B.S. Rowntree. *Poverty. A Study of Town Life. London*, 1901, p. 116.
38. David Vincent, *Poor Citizens: The State and the Poor in Twentieth-Century Britain*, Longman, London & New York, 1991, p. 3.
39. Advertisement, *Evening Mail*, 27.19.99.
40. Flyer advertising Helen Butcher, The Treacle Stick, Quercus, Warwick, 1999.
41. Flyer for The Treacle Stick.
42. Fira Bibi Ali. *My Roots* (unpublished mss.).1999.
43. Douglas V. Jones. *Memories of a Twenties Child*, Westwood Press Publications, Sutton Coldfield, 1995, p. 37.
44. See James Caffrey, 'We teach them far too much, too young' (Letter) in *Evening Mail*, 15.10.99, page 11. B. Dunn, 'The Hard Sell' (Letter) in *Evening Mail*, 20.9.99, p. 10. Maureen Messant (Leader) 'Why Our Future's Looking So Ugly' in *Evening Mail*, 2.10.99, p. 6. For a liberal reaction see Christopher Anton. 'Fight for Rights' (Letter) in *Evening Mail*, 15.10.99, p. 10.
45. Mrs B. Browning 'Good to be non-PC' (Letter) in *Evening Mail*, 25.10.99.
46. Mrs Hawkesford quoted in Carl Chinn, 'Going through an odd phase' in *Evening Mail*, 7.8.99, p.19.
47. Paul Murtagh, (Letter) in *Evening Mail*, 11.10.99, p. 10.
48. Mike Davey (Letter) in *Evening Mail*, 5.10.99, p. 16.
49. I own up to being one of these correspondents but for a more objective example see Reg Finn, (Letter) in *Evening Mail*, 28.9.99, p. 10.
50. Ivan Karp. 'Introduction. Museums and Communities: The Politics of Public Culture' in Ivan Karp, Christine Muller Kreamer & Steven D. Lavine (eds) *Museums and Communities: The Politics of Public Culture*, Smithsonian Institution Press, Washington & London, 1992.
51. For a discussion of this site see Jane Peirson Jones. 'The Colonial Legacy and the Community: the Gallery 33 Project' in Ivan Karp, Christine Muller Kreamer & Steven D. Lavine (eds) *Museums and Communities: The Politics of Public Culture*, Smithsonian Institution Press, Washington and London, 1992.
52. Birmingham City Council. Department of Leisure and Community Services, *The Brumillennium Project: Bringing Birmingham's History to Life*, (Summary of the Brumillennium Project), 1999, p. 1.
53. Ibid.
54. Ibid.
55. Helen Lloyd, personal communication, 8.11.99. The programme referred to was 'Belonging', The Century Speaks. BBC Radio WM, TX. 3.10.99.
56. Carol Kammen 'On Doing Local History' in *Local History Magazine*, No. 53, Jan/Feb 1996, p. 13.

Photograph of the Bishopsgate Institute in advance of its formal opening in 1894

Managing boundaries: history and community at the Bishopsgate Institute[1]

Peter Claus

City types, local 'characters' and academics still seek out the reference library of the Bishopsgate Institute. As a confluence for these diverse groups, it is also a repository for Public History and lifelong learning in two interlocking ways. First, the George Jacob Holyoake (1817–1906) and the George Howell (1833–1910) papers are collections of national and international significance, though like the Bradlaugh material and archive of the National Secular Society, they might be read as local testimonies. The London collection is important, as is that of the London Co-operative Society covering local societies in Greater London from the mid-nineteenth century, as well as the library of the east London anarchist organisation, the Freedom Press. Second, the Bishopsgate Institute is a natural home for family and community history. Whether it be a search for heritage in the City or 'roots' in the East End, it brings together amateur and professional, antiquarian and trained historian.

The Institute as a whole also provides a point of interaction for formal and informal knowledge, for that contained in 'official' documents and so on and for the mediating interventions of local knowledge and memory. Most of the users are City workers, but others are drawn from the East End and beyond. Sixth-formers swot for examinations or pursue a school project and the homeless or marginal sit in the warm to wile away the hours. Its manuscript archive and its unique London collections, along with its extensive educational programme, make it a spot where past and present are in constant negotiation. Public History at the Bishopsgate Institute, in this guise at least, is a social form of knowledge. Raphael Samuel, in the first volume of *Theatres of Memory* defined Public History in a way that works well for understanding the Institute's all-encompassing educational role. Public History is, he argued, 'those community-based, work- or office related, and institutional forms of historical self-presentation and display which serve alike for affirming minority identities and boosting corporate images'.[2] Different community heritages, from the East End and the City, geographical boundaries, political boundaries and boundaries concerned with gender and class all abut at the Bishopsgate Institute. How, as an endowed charity, it managed and manages these boundaries is vital for a deeper understanding of its workings.

The management of these boundaries has involved an essential compromise. This is expressed in an architecture that is very much of the 1890s, a fruit of the marriage between the traditionalism and the progressivism of the Arts and Crafts movement and a sibling of an advanced Art Nouveau. Appropriately, it was born, or rather planted, at the edge of the City of London, itself an energetic expression of modernity at the *fin de siècle*. Even 'planted' does not quite convey the organic metamorphosis from moribund parochial charities connected to the district into a place of learning, leisure and welfare.[3] Erected and equipped for £78, 625, and designed by the architect Charles Harrison Townsend (1851–1928), it made tangible the principles of the Arts and Crafts Movement, with learning and useful work seen essentially as recreation.[4]

The Bishopsgate Institute is located three-quarters in the City of London and one quarter in East London and until recently the boundary line could be traced through the former lending library. This line is hugely important to the Institute's historical self-perception and influences the type of public passing through its buff terracotta facade, into its more ornamentally Romanesque interior. Spatially, it is organised into a library that houses an array of important collections and a Hall that is still the site of recitals and lectures, but is now more likely to host professional examinations. Since its founding in the 1890s it has undergone many changes, including the

Seeing History: Public History in Britain Now 153

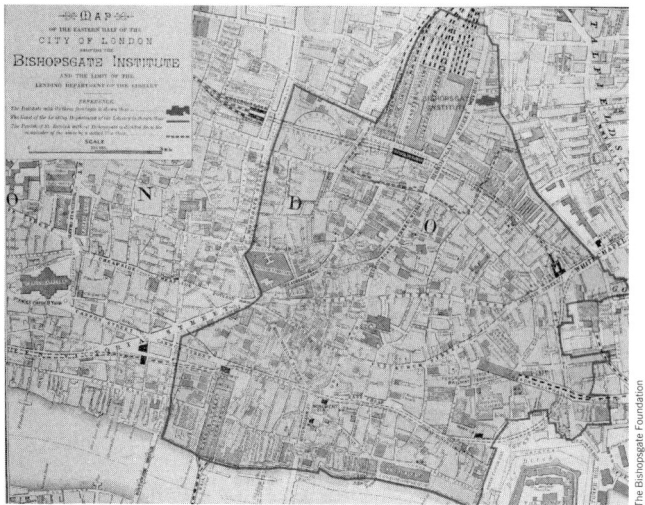

Map of the eastern half of the City of London showing the Bishopsgate Institute and the limit of the Lending Department of the Library, 1894

installation of a magnificent organ in 1913 and a restaurant in 1945, both now sadly gone. War damage took its toll and a timber and glass screen replaced the original exterior bronze gates in the 1960s. It has had a recent centenary makeover, thanks to Lottery funding, which made possible the acquisition of an eighteenth-century building – the Brushfield wing. All the while, the Institute has welcomed pensioners associated with the area – latter-day supplicants of the parochial charities – providing them with a small quarterly allowance, trips out of London, regular tea and sympathy, and opportunities to reminisce.[5] Its bold architectural style borrowed from many eras and genres express the open and cosmopolitan nature of a building that apparently from the first held little awe for City and East End denizen alike; more than once in the early years it was mistaken for a railway station, a roller-skating rink, and even a matrimonial agency.[6] Resistance to symmetry, imaginatively and symbolically, informs its educational, leisure and welfare roles.

Facing two ways: geographical boundaries

Historically, it is likely that the Bishopsgate Institute was always balanced on the cusp of many boundaries. It is critical to know from where the Institute attracted its users. It was never, I think, a natural port of call for those new to Britain. In the 1890s Yiddish was more likely to have been heard at the nearby Banford library, off the Mile End Road, or, alternatively, as someone who spent his Jewish boyhood here suggested, at the Whitechapel library.[7] Similarly, Toynbee Hall, founded on Christmas Eve 1884, had as its educational rationale the construction of a new moral world.[8] In contrast the Institute has been less evangelising, less concerned with social reform, offering pleasurable education to a fluid population in the streets around its front door; streets still teeming with finance workers and those who service the City's infrastructure.

To appreciate fully the breadth of this appeal it ought to be understood that now, as in the past, the City has its share of casual or marginal workers; 'City gents' have never dominated it. Many see the square mile exclusively as a breeding ground for the bowler hatted, pinstripe suburban suit or, more recently still, as a playground for the stockbroker with a Tudor mansion in Surrey. This is quite misplaced. Despite the apparent novelty of the boom-time slickers of the 1980s, unruly behaviour was already a feature of the City by the 1890s, as testified by a complaint made by early library assistants at the Institute.[9] It is likewise wrong to view the City, and therefore the Institute's public, as a habitat for the deferential clerk, Pooter.[10] Under-reported in nineteenth-century historiography are socialistic clerks in City offices, where a short-lived national Union was formed and a Prudential Agent was dismissed for attending the Trade Union Congress.[11] Even within the Bank of England, where the rules were broken by playing the stock and share market in order to augment meagre salaries, 'drunkenness' accompanied 'unpolished' table manners.[12] Mrs Robert Henrey picked her way through post-second world war City bombsites and acknowledged its cosmopolitan nature. She observed 'coal-black' West Indians, like earlier Victorian Jewish petty traders or German clerks, driven metaphorically at least to the City's imaginative margins.[13] Technological changes, such as the introduction of the typewriter in the 1890s, meant that 'young toughs' working at its heart, along with its minorities and outsiders, were eventually joined by female labour.[14] Women made 'the City look brighter' and were early visitors to the Bishopsgate Institute. Yet women, like the working class and the ethnic minorities, appear as extras to the more imperious drama of the City. Even now there is a perception that it is dominated by very masculine excitement, and in recent years, sexual adventure. But this too is quite wrong and understates the informal economy of the area and the legion of workers that historically serviced it.

One justification for this perception is the idea of the City as bereft of community. This impression is reinforced by the decline of the City's residential population during the last half of the nineteenth century. It is true to say that by the 1890s population in the City was dipping and had done so in each decennial year after 1851. But City-wide, its depletion was mostly at the heart, not the periphery.[15] Comparing the central wards of the City with the outer wards, such as Bishopsgate Without, we find that the population decrease was not always sudden or continuous. Indeed there were more people living in some of the outer wards by the end of the century than at its mid-point. Population did not haemorrhage from the centre of the City, nor did it leak from the edges. In fact, people slipped in and out, or 'flitted' to use a contemporary term. Bishopsgate, or 'Costermongria' to give it its late-Victorian nickname, was a district generally advanced in sanitary matters, but one nevertheless that suffered from high mortality levels and overcrowding, suffering too from a fluctuating population.[16] Between 1881 and 1891 the residential population in Bishopsgate, mostly women, dropped by 1,885. If the total residential parish population was 4,983 in 1881 and 3,078 a decade later, the day census figures record a greater stability: 19,645 came into this area on one day in 1881 and 19,848 in 1891. Of these, only 2,889 were women (there were almost as many children) in 1881, and in 1891 the proportion was even smaller at 1,346.[17] Overcrowding rates in the City generally were more than the national average: population density in 1851 averaged 180 per acre, 131 in the centre, and 291 in the poorer western and eastern areas such as Bishopsgate.[18] Here, in 1881 and 1891, overcrowding was severe at 9.83 and 9.71 per dwelling respectively.[19] The City was not, therefore, without residents at night or during the weekend, nor quite yet totally dominated by middle-class, male finance workers during daylight hours.

One important contemporary commentator was William Rogers, rector of St Botolph, Bishopsgate.[20] As an active Liberal and passionate advocate for secular education he certainly knew the daily realities of the resident population and bore witness to human tragedy in the most immoral neighbourhood he had ever known. Merchants previously living over counting houses had removed to desirable suburban neighbourhoods. Towards the east, replacing the weavers, metal-founders and leather-dressers, was an enormous wool warehouse. Here lived a different kind of City slicker, whose presence was as important to its economic well-being as any financier or banker. According to Rogers, there were 'boot-translators', 'slop-tailors', 'office-cleaners', and 'street-sellers' ('men who trade in baked potatoes in winter and "hokey-pokey" – a mysterious compound in summer'). These, plus 'an indescribable lot who prefer to do odd jobs', were largely hidden off the courts and alleys of the grander thoroughfare of Bishopsgate, where much of the City's more conventional business was carried on. Rogers thought many of his parishioners, whether Irish Catholic, Jewish, or Quaker, in addition to Anglicans and other Dissenters, needed a whole staff of sanitary inspectors to attend to their needs. Or even better, he believed, railways or roads should clear a path through the rookeries. Not necessarily waiting to be 'improved', the resident population began to disperse eastwards in the 1890s at the very moment that the parochial charities that had partially maintained them were rationalised.

One reason for the building of the Bishopsgate Institute was as a response to this human tragedy – a response to poverty that did not involve a distribution of doles. Another was the general refurbishment of Bishopsgate's public places. The White Hart public house in the district retained a basic service: no food, no tables and standing room only, but others improved with the clientele. 'Dirty Dick's', partially rebuilt in the 1870s, an early example of a 'heritage' pub rebuilt to a theme, had a non-smoking policy and sported mummified cats, stuffed rats and strategically placed cobwebs. Not least because of its obvious respectability, it became known as 'Clean Richard's'. Crosby Hall, once a place for young men's evening classes, now entertained well-heeled diners. The classes from 1860 moved to Sussex Hall, Leadenhall Street, eventually becoming the City of London College.[21] One upshot of the modernisation of the built environment was the Bishopsgate Institute with the splendid 'Hang Theology' Rogers (so-called because of his approach to secular reform and his rejection of theory without praxis) as its leading light. He was also its first Chairman of Governors. It was Rogers who famously said that he wished to turn flannel petticoats into a Free Library, a reference to an ancient and now superfluous allowance willed to poor women by long dead citizens of the neighbourhood.

Despite obvious need, support for the establishment of the Bishopsgate Institute within the City was initially lukewarm. Their functions usurped, the popular based nurseries of citizenship, the Wardmotes and Inquest Committees had effectively disappeared by 1856. In their stead, associations like the Bishopsgate Club, revived in 1860, reflected a shift from participatory political structures native to the City, to governance by organisations grafted on to the City and by those connected by work rather than residency. Like the Bishopsgate Ratepayers Association, they based notions of citizenship on property not residency, and sunk differences with fine wine rather than acrid debate.[22] The new City-wide associations merged defence of the constitution with the protection of property and stood ideologically against the encroaching power of mass democracy. They were likely to give allegiance to the Cobden Club or, expressing an individualist bent, align themselves with the Liberty and Property Defence League, the London Chamber of Commerce or the Navy League. Unsurprisingly, the Bishopsgate Ward Club appeared indifferent to the foundation of the Institute: minutes are silent on the matter. The members did though have views on the Fabian Society's Eight-Hour Day Bill coming before Parliament. One thought it 'absurd' and another 'idiotic'. A local representative, Common Councillor Greenaway, believed the Fabian Society to be 'the biggest lot of jackasses in creation'. Another 'hoped that in future the Club would be freed from discussion relating to the Fabian Society'.[23] However, proposals for an eight-hour day was still a hot topic when Prime Minister Lord Rosebery came to lay the foundation stone in 1893. There was an inherent tension between a wish to provide education for self-improvement aimed at the respectable and deserving and a need to provide pastimes for the many. Initially, despite City doubts, it was with an appeal to the many that this young establishment defined itself.

Blue Books and biscuits
Prime Minister Lord Rosebery outlined to whom he believed the Institute should appeal:

> And if the Bishopsgate Institute draws within its circle only those who are already capable of profiting by books, pictures, concerts, classes and scientific meetings, it will only be one more such establishment among a host of not very notably successful competitors. It will not be what it ought to be – a real charity as well as an adaptation of charities; a chief exponent of the insurpassable [sic] charity of filling up lives of which, according to the eight hours work 'stanza', a full third in many cases remain empty.[24]

Here the emphasis, amid agitation for a limited working day, is on leisure as the basis for the Institute, not education for citizenship as at the Mechanics Institute or that creature of the 1900s, the Workers Education Association. Rosebery's well-received oration, spoken amid much ceremony and before every important educator of the day, argued for the needs of 'great masses of the people', in mind and in body, and was a message well taken.[25] His mantra that life could not be reduced to a 'blue book and biscuit' – a parliamentary blue book for mental activity and a biscuit to sustain physical needs – was something taken to heart by the Institute, at least at first.[26] Useful knowledge or 'Really Useful Knowledge' was not enough to feed the soul.

Others, at least in the City, did not attempt to mix education with amusement and had built museums and libraries with the ratepayer, not the masses, in mind. This, despite the efforts of the City's' most eminent antiquarian, Charles Roach Smith (1807-1890), a numismatist and stalwart of many of Britain's archaeological societies.[27] As a young man, he worked in a wholesale warehouse at Snow Hill in the City of London. Later he lived at Lothbury at the corner of Founders' Court and behind the Bank of England. From this vantage point he led a team of young enthusiasts who were attempting to preserve tessellated pavements, sculptures and the like from the heavy tread of City improvements. As a reward for his work he was greeted by the City of London Corporation, the ancient local authority of the square mile, with a mixture of 'great apathy', 'rude and studied obstinacy', and even persecution.[28] Indeed, he brought an action against them when they sought to evict him, eventually finding himself at an address in Liverpool Street, Bishopsgate, somewhat poorer, and with his collection of artefacts permanently dispersed. But he continued to argue for the cause of conservation in the City,[29] campaigning to find a permanent home for his collections and to establish a museum of City antiquities. He offered to sell the result of half a lifetime's work to the Corporation, at an independently adjudicated price. Characteristically rejected by the ratepayers on the grounds of cost at a meeting held at the Mansion House in November 1855, he saw his hopes for a museum dashed. Not surprisingly, perhaps, he reacted angrily. 'The decision of the meeting was really a very fair expression of the state of mind of the majority of the shopocracy of the City. If the sentiments of the industrious artisans, of the clerks, of the prentices, and of the youth of the City, who are not ratepayers, could have had weight, a free museum would have been voted forthwith.'[30]

The City Corporation had the ratepayer in mind when it built a resplendent new library in 1873. The first library, built between 1824 and 1828, housed 2,800 volumes and a free circulating library was introduced in the mid-1850s. Annual attendance had climbed from 14,316 in 1868 in the old library to 173,559 by 1874 in the new one. The collection held 50,000 books by the time the warehousemen, traders and their employees petitioned in 1876 – partly fulfilling the prophecy made by Roach Smith – for the library to be kept open until nine o'clock every evening, except Saturday.[31] By this time, a museum in Basinghall Street also proved a popular attraction. It expanded from just one room in 1840 and was home to Roman finds that the City was constantly yielding and that Roach Smith had worked so tirelessly to rescue.

Political, class and gender boundaries
What the function of the new Bishopsgate Institute should be, therefore, seemed to be a question asked, if not fully answered. To whom it catered, similarly, remained a problem. Problems of demarcation touched on issues of politics as well as class and gender boundaries. We can see the heavy influence in the early years of the Arts and Crafts Movement and the labour movement. Walter Crane designed the library bookplate and when William Morris died his widow donated two

Bishopsgate Library bookplate by Walter Crane circa 1894

of his romances printed by the Kelmscott Press. These sympathies continued into the Edwardian period when, in 1907, Ramsay Macdonald was a participant at the two week long Clarion Guild of Handicraft Exhibition held in the Hall at Bishopsgate.[32] The interdependence of work and leisure, analogous to the Institute's mission as articulated by Rosebery at its founding moment, happened also to be part of the Arts and Crafts message. In 1907, as secretary of the Labour party, Macdonald gave a sum of money to the Institute, as did various other branches of the infant labour movement. The archives of both Howell and Holyoake were deposited there in 1905 and 1906. In 1911, Will Crooks, one of Labour's local heroes in Woolwich, journeying from 'Workhouse to Westminster', gave a lecture at the Institute, while speakers like Graham Wallas lectured on radical themes well into the years of the First World War. Yet in the 1920s, the Governors locked up the Minute Book of the First International Working-Men's Association, 1866-69. They also banned the *Socialist Standard* from the newsroom in 1922, having already hosted meetings of right-wing organisations like the Navy League. Perhaps this is evidence of pressure from more conservative elements in the City, becoming increasingly influential in the Institute's affairs.

In 1893 when the laying of the foundation stone took place, Professor Bryce, MP, saw the Institute as a meeting point for the lonely and displaced. He was thinking particularly of strangers in London: 'After all, the best kind of education and amusement was that which they gave each other in friendship.'[33] Indeed this has been just one honourable and humanitarian service provided by the Institute, with regular readers coming from the nearby Salvation Army Hostel.[34] The *City Press* in 1893 thought the Institute was intended 'for the moral and intellectual benefit of the poorer classes of the eastern part of the City and the East End generally' and that it should be a 'People's Palace'. At the same time, it should also cater for office workers on the 'Eastern fringe' of the City.[35] By far the largest group numerically in the early years were commercial clerks, but typists and fishmongers, solicitors and cleaners, teachers and shop assistants all made their presence felt. There was even a manufacturer of tennis bats, representing the workshops that were still part of the City economy in the 1890s.

As for women, they were segregated and in a minority. Out of 1,617 daily readers in the newsroom on one October day in 1907, only 68 were female.[36] It seems probable that women were more likely to take books home and minimise time spent in what was a largely male domain. They were also less likely to consult journals and advertising sheets. An early decision not to establish a separate boy's reading room meant that, with exceptions, such as a children's lecture in 1901 and the Puffin Club in the 1980s, the Institute has not accommodated the very young. This too might well have limited access to the Institute by women whose family commitments were a major consideration.

There were tensions involved in managing the Institute. Heard loud and clear, business voices complained about the time it took to consult a book or a journal when it eventually opened to the public in 1894. The queues to enter the place were too long, the shelves too high and borrowing time, too short.[37] There were also, it seems, jitters at the unusual proximity of rich and poor, women and men. Certainly, the corridor was often jammed solid and was, despite the long wait, a place of fascination. Here the eager reader could find notices posted, or amble along memory lane with sketches of parts of old London destroyed by the railways or other improvements. Great favourites, however, were the imperial maps that used pin flags to chart the progress of the armies of the Empire. Other maps illustrated areas of the Colonies that now provided new homes for friends and relatives of those left at home in Bishopsgate or its environs.[38] In short, this was a site of social transgression. On at least one occasion, 'improper' bodily contact and the violation of what we might term 'personal space' led to complaints aimed directly at the Institute. Exposed along this ten foot wide corridor running the length of the building, social relations and History, certainly Local History, became an issue of popular contest and debate. It was also at that time, recalling Raphael Samuel, a place of 'historical self-presentation' and visual 'display'. The newly appointed librarian must certainly have felt these pressures upon appointment in 1897.

Prospero's books
The Institute's librarian Charles William Frederick Goss (1864–1946) inherited a Free Library with open access to its

shelves and with a mixed public knocking on his door, or rather packing his corridor. His personality was to dominate the Bishopsgate Library until his retirement in 1941. He was a giant in his field and was responsible for bringing the major manuscript collections to the Institute as well as beginning a fine Local History collection enhanced under David Webb's stewardship from 1966 until his recent retirement. Goss was responsible for the inauguration of the Society for Public Libraries, formed in opposition to the established Library Association of the United Kingdom. His opposition was brought about by the neglect of metropolitan libraries in particular.[39] He was also a member of the London and Middlesex Archaeological Society, eventually serving as Vice-President. In 1919, he was elected as a Fellow of the Society of Antiquaries. He was also the author of some important books on local history, with a particular expertise in trade directories. Apparently, he had a radical streak, and wrote antiquarian pieces for the *Newcastle Weekly Chronicle*, then under the editorship of the old Chartist, W. E. Adams, and later maintaining a relationship of trust with Robert Applegarth and George Howell.[40]

His first act as librarian of the Bishopsgate Institute, however, a year after his appointment in 1897, was to argue for a closed access system that was to serve a public made up of a delimited type of City worker. Labelled because of this single act, a 'reactionary', there is no doubt that contemporary criticism touched a nerve.[41] In fact, one dispute linked to this matter led to legal proceedings and an out of court settlement. His opponents, and they were many, claimed the numbers of readers had fallen. In reply, he argued that under the open shelf system the numbers waiting in the library corridor to gain entry led to inefficiencies. By 1901, a smaller staff dealt with enquiries quicker, the number of stolen books was dramatically reduced and in any case, he said, the change had removed 'idlers in the library'.[42] This reference to 'idlers' was at complete variance with the ideal of the Institute as a place of education, leisure and fellowship. Being 'idle' in the Bishopsgate library, reading a book or journal, or attending this or that entertainment or lecture in its Hall precisely fulfilled its mission. In like manner, there was an obvious attempt to narrow the class range by making overtures to the City, targeting its needs as a place of business. This alone was a departure from the founding principles of the Institute. No surprise, then, that of the total number of 4,887 book borrowers from the City, 1,045, the lion's share, came from the Bishopsgate Without ward on its periphery. By 1899 and in the years after, 1910 is representative, only a few hundred more came from places termed 'other districts'. It was also a retreat from a mediating position between the varying demands of City and East End. One way for Goss to seal this change was to control the reading material. Another was to aim the educational programme at a City audience that worked, but did not live in the area.

From idle reading to leisurely study
A calamity befell the Institute in 1896 when Rogers, its guiding star, died. This came after a blow the previous November when the Positivist Frederic Harrison prescribed what he considered the proper choice of books:

I do believe that nearly half of our actual reading today is either positively injurious, or at least utterly useless. The good books to read are so many, the mountains of rubbish are so vast, and the fatty degeneration of the brain caused by reading is so common – that some care, some selection of our books, is a moral duty that we owe to ourselves, our homes, and the societies in which we live.[43]

Degeneration, very much a concept of the 1890s, found itself mentioned in the same breath with 'idle reading'. Harrison was at particular pains to please his City audience and to highlight the lack of 'time for reading at the disposal of the busy man'.[44] Fiction reading among the poor and feckless was a cause of moral panic in many Free Libraries and Bishopsgate was no exception.[45] In 1896, Goss' predecessor, Ronald Heaton, argued that fiction made up a low percentage of the total of books consulted and defended the open system –– 'allowing them to select books themselves'.[46] Goss contested this, reporting to the Governors in 1898 that he thought the percentage of fiction reading high, but that 'scientific works and books of a more solid character are taken out for purposes of study and for longer'. He continued:

...unless one had the power of directing the minds of the members into regular study, it is probable that the suppression of light reading would but make fewer instead of better readers, and thus drive many to less carefully selected stores than those on the shelves of the Institute. While the undue use of works of imagination has its claim as well as the more utilitarian faculties, and that people employed in the active business of life require their imagination to be raised and stirred.[47]

By closing the shelves Goss not only removed choice but also drove readers, some local readers at least, elsewhere. Issues by the lending library in 1901–1902 (the year the closed system began) totalled 140,001, and in 1914 a miserly 103,389. In the reference library the number of issues during 1903, the year after the introduction of the closed system, registered 23,875 and in 1914 recorded only a modest increase to, 29,268. This when the total numbers of books in stock for reference purposes went up from 8,600 to 23,477 over the same period. Favourite reading in the reference library included the *Gentleman's Magazine* and Farrar's *Life of Christ*. When the Great War broke out this list extended to include some more imperialistic titles, such as W.J. Pincombe's *Britain and the Gallant Belgium*. The explorer Ernest Shackleton had already planted the flag for Empire in 1910 when he 'packed the Hall to capacity – at 2s 6d for back seats and 5s for stalls'.[48] Indeed the Institute rallied to both flag and Empire by opening a recreation room for servicemen back from the Front in 1914–1918 and likewise did its bit in 1939–1945 by acting as an ambulance station.

These figures are important because they suggest another departure from the founding principles of the Institute. The business City as a constituency was becoming more important. No surprise then, that the number of visits to the Newsroom was 290, 936 in 1901 (only 10,693 were women), but rose to half a million in 1914. Freely consulted were journals dealing with the infrastructure of the market. Following the same pattern, numbers attending the evening lectures (a draw for those who lived locally) was 7,263 in 1901–1902, but only 6,651 in 1914. By contrast, lunchtime attendance (for those who worked locally) stood at 2,700 at the beginning of the period and stood at a massive 20,232 by the end. By 1911, the Institute could boast 'material representing trade interests and every phase of science and thought'. There was a special emphasis 'on guides of almost every part of the globe'. Hall-based activities included a musical society (100 members), a physical culture class and lunch-hour concerts with 'each performance being attended by 450 persons'.[49] Under the guiding hand of Goss, the Bishopsgate Institute was attracting the 'cream of the lecturing platform' — Hilaire Belloc was one high profile speaker, George Sims, another. Goss also developed short vocational courses. In 1898, there were courses given in French (101 registered), shorthand (84), book keeping (67), commercial arithmetic (31), music (85), voice production (32) and first aid (44).[50]

Nevertheless, there were continuities as well as changes. The emphasis was always, as befitting its Arts and Crafts pedigree, on training as pleasure. The Rev. C.H. Grundy, for example, gave a lecture in 1899 on the 'Social effects of the Bicycle Upon The New Man, The New Woman And The New Child', along with his 'numerous anecdotes of cycling'.[51] But the audience attracted was very much, according to Goss, 'the higher and more educated classes', the events designed, by his own admission, 'for the use of persons who have little or no leisure for study'.[52] Goss also brought positive change: this ambitious cultural and educational programme would, over the years, bring much kudos to the Institute and bring it closer to the imaginative nerve centre of national sentiment. By the 1930s, recitals attracted a diverse audience from the City and elsewhere, although City workers predominated. One correspondent for the *Spectator*, Gilbert Thomas, described the audience attending a 'luncheon hour' organ recital by the resident organist, Reginald Goss-Custard:

> They were extraordinarily varied; but the most striking feature, next to the few very old men, who themselves seemed to have strayed back to earth from a previous existence, was the number of young City clerks of both sexes, particularly the male, who evidently preferred a hasty sandwich followed by good music to a proper lunch and gossip or dominoes at a restaurant.[53]

Later the Bishopsgate Institute attracted major names to its live and recorded radio broadcasts. Myra Hess was a famous contributor and the political current affairs programme Question Time was broadcast from the Institute in 1983, featuring David Steel and Denis Healey.

'Co-existence'

The Institute's Spring 2000 prospectus, *Education at the Heart of the City*, offers 'short courses for City workers', at 'lunchtime and after work' and all 'minutes from your office'. Its courses taught by some impressive specialists are typically varied. 'Dress for Success: A Two Part Course For Women' or 'Juggling and Other Disorganised Buffoonery' are only two examples, alongside others in languages, literature and art appreciation. The Institute's motto 'I grow old if I cease to learn' is well expressed in its educational programme. Mindful of the disparate communities it serves, the Bishopsgate Foundation (as the Institute's governing body) is currently undertaking a major remodelling of its services and is committed to meeting changing educational demands and the challenges of new technology. In another recent prospectus, it has pledged 'A remodelled Institute [that] enables us to continue a long tradition of providing educational and cultural opportunities to the people of East London, the City and far beyond'. Able to respond to change, to find 'a bridge to the past', it is returning to its first principles – a duality articulated over the years – to provide pleasure and instruction in equal measure.[54] Other boundaries have settled differently.

Geographically, the Bishopsgate Institute faces the edge of the City's financial heart and looks up at the Bishopsgate and Broadgate developments, built between 1986 and 1994 at the cost of £800 million. Interestingly, Raphael Samuel reporting some of the delights of the Bishopsgate Institute stated boldly that it was in the East End.[55] In fact, since he wrote this warm tribute for the *History Workshop Journal* in 1978, the City has moved further east. Where once prostitutes and 'street Arabs' patrolled outside the Institute in the Edwardian era and even recently were a feature of the eastern perimeters of Spitalfields Market, they have now begun to ebb further into what is indisputably the East End. Caught by this City tide, the Brushfield Street side entrance of the Institute leading to Spitalfields – an area home to waves of immigrants – is closed to the public and serves as an entrance for staff. Political boundaries have altered accordingly and it is quite often to the City that the Institute looks for funding and support, a salutary fact that influences, in turn, the class and gender boundaries that oscillate within its walls.

For Raphael Samuel the special value of the Institute was 'not the existence of this or that collection' but rather, as he put it, 'the co-existence, under one roof, of historical sources which normally exist in separate spheres'.[56] Also of huge consequence is the vital mix or 'co-existence' of people and types that will ensure the Institute's future. Whether amateur or professional, retrieving 'official' knowledge or not, it relies on a juxtaposition of sources and people, not the victory of one element over another. On the contrary, the presence of each ensures the vitality of the other. Raphael Samuel articulated this essential balance or 'co-existence' between sources and mediators, while underlining the strengths of this balance at the Institute. It has a '...peculiar mix of the everyday and the bizarre, the antiquarian and the contemporary, the solid and the ephemeral.' A mix, he continued, 'which has shaped my own *Theatres of Memory*.'[57] Fittingly, the Raphael Samuel Centre for Metropolitan History, based at Bishopsgate, maintains an interdisciplinary focus while fostering links with local historians and non-academics. Strengthened immeasurably by the recent acquisition of the Raphael Samuel archive itself, the Institute has an all-embracing approach to public education, and one that manages difficult borderlands. Offering leisure and education it provides intellectual 'milk and beef tea', as well as affording actual sustenance for local pensioners. It has a clear idea of its role, a role that gives service and even shows affection for a mixed community drawn from across many boundaries and fulfilling, therefore, a modern function consistent with its founding principles.

Notes

1. I was given full and free access to the Bishopsgate Institute's own archive and a chance to work on George Howell's desk. For both acts of kindness, I thank all the library staff at the Institute, particularly the Chief Librarian Alice Mackay and the Senior Library Assistant, Jeff Abbott.
2. Raphael Samuel, *Theatres of Memory. Past and Present in Contemporary Culture*, Verso, London, 1994, p. 278.
3. Victor Belcher, *The City Parochial Foundation 1891–1991*, Scolar Press, Aldershot, 1991.
4. This description is taken from the following: Peter Guillery, 'Bishopsgate Institute and Library (includes No.6 Brushfield Street)', Royal Commission on the Historical Monuments of England, November 1995; Simon Bradley and Nikolaus Pevsner, *London 1: The City of London*, Penguin, Harmondsworth, 1997; Edwina Burness, 'The Bishopsgate Institute: Past and Present', *Bishopsgate News*, 1984.
5. Brenda Squires recently put together the reminiscence project at the Bishopsgate Institute 'Do you remember?' attended by senior citizens in the Bishopsgate area. See, for example, Isobel Barker, A Friend of the Bishopsgate Institute in Conversation with Geoffrey Ince and Bob Roberts, Tuesday 12 August 1997 (privately printed by the Institute). The last available figures for the Foundation's charitable expenditure on pensioners shows 47 senior citizens using £2,400 on lunches, taking four excursions at £2,000 and receiving quarterly pensions amounting to £77 each. A further £24,500 was spent on

annual grants to local charities, making a total annual expenditure of £43,376. The Institute started with 118 pensioners in 1891 spending £1,265 but this soon reduced to 39, less than now, and an outlay of £1,014. These figures exclude the separate Emergency Fund and the early employment of an outreach nurse.
6   *Daily Telegraph*, 27 February 1899.
7   The author was in conversation with the late David Englander.
8   The Open University Arts Fourth Level Course, A427 CD-ROM, 'Charles Booth and Social Investigation in Nineteenth Century Britain'. Toynbee Hall was a 'workstation' for Charles Booth and his team and a 'centre for social action which combined social research and observation with social, philanthropic and educational work within the community of the East End'. See also, David Englander and Rosemary O'Day (eds.), *Retrieved Riches. Social Investigation in Britain 1850-1914*, Scolar Press, Aldershot, 1994.
9   David Webb, *Bishopsgate Foundation Centenary History* (Published by the Governors of the Bishopsgate Foundation, 1991) p. 12.
10 George & Weedon Grossmith, *Diary of a Nobody*, Wordsworth Classics, Hertfordshire, 1994.
11 Guildhall Library. (Manuscripts) Ms. 20, 383 Diary of Andrew Carlyle Tait; Born in 1878, his father kept a bookshop in the City. The family moved to Ilford, Essex when Tait began his diary in 1893-4. However, he returned to the City as an apprentice to John Spicer and Co., 50 Thames Street.
12 Allan Fea, *Recollections of Sixty Years*, The Richards Press, London, 1927; Fea started work in the Bank of England in 1881 and was a noted antiquarian.
13 Mrs Robert Henrey, T*he Virgin of Aldermanbury. Rebirth of the City of London*, Dent, London, 1958, p. 192.
14 Even now, the transition is incomplete. Messengers, often ex-servicemen, scurrying from one office to the next, have disappeared to be replaced by the fashion-conscious bicycle courier.
15 Karl Guntar Grytzell, *County of London – Population Changes 1801–1901* Swedish Royal University, Dept of Geography, Lund, 1969, p. 87.
16 *St James Budget*, 24 January 1896.
17 (Public Record Office) *Census of England and Wales 1851–1891*; J Salmon, *Ten Year Growth of the City of London. Report of the Day Census (1891)*.
18 Royston Lambert, *Sir John Simon, 1816-1904, and English Social Administration*, MacGibbon & Kee, London, 1963, p. 86.
19 These figures are from Peter Claus, 'Real Liberals' and Conservatives in the City of London 1848-1886 (Open University, Unpublished Ph.D., 1998), Volume 2, Appendix 1.
20 The following is from R.H. Haddon, *Reminiscences of William Rogers, Rector of St. Botolph Bishopsgate*, Kegan Paul, Trench & Co., London, 1888.
21 Edward Callow, *Old London Taverns – Historical, Descriptive and Reminiscent, with Some Account of the Coffee Houses, Clubs etc.*, Downey, London, 1899, p. 63.
22 For more on City popular politics in the 1850s and beyond see Peter Claus, 'Languages of Citizenship in the City of London 1848-1867', *London Journal*, Vol. 24, Number 1, June 1999.
23 G.L. (Mans) Ms. 5127 Minutes of the Bishopsgate Ward Club, Wednesday, 10 December 1890.
24 *The Globe*, 15 May 1893.
25 *Daily News*, 14 May 1893.
26 *Observer*, 14 May 1893

27 Charles Roach Smith, *Retrospections, Social and Archaeological,* printed by subscription, London, 1883.
28 Henry Smetham, *C.R.S. and His Friends – Being Personal Recollections of Charles Roach Smith and his Friends*, London, 1929, p. 19.
29 Public Dinner given to C. Roach Smith, at Newport, Isle of Wight on Tuesday, August 28, 1855, London, 1855.
30 Quoted in Brian Hobley, 'Charles Roach Smith (1807-1890) Pioneer Rescue Archaeologist', *The London Archaeologist*, 2, (1975), xiii, p. 330, n.6.
31 Charles Welch, *Modern History of the City of London. A Record of Municipal and Social Progress from 1760 to the Present Day*, Blades, East & Blades, London, 1896, p. 292.
32 *Daily News*, September 1907; *Morning Leader*, September 1907; *Daily Chronicle*, 25 September, 1907.
33 *City Press*, Wednesday 17 May 1893.
34 Raphael Samuel, 'The Bishopsgate Institute', *History Workshop Journal*, No.5, 1978, pp. 164-172
35 *City Press*, Wednesday 17 May 1893
36 The following figures are held in the Bishopsgate Foundation's own archive and are from the Bishopsgate Foundation Report of the Governing Body 1896-1914
37 *City Press*, 27 March, 1895
38 *London Argus*, 2 November 1900.
39 Minutes of the Proceedings of a Meeting of the Society of Public Libraries held at the Bishopsgate Institute on Wednesday November 17, 1897.
40 See Raphael Samuel, 'The Bishopsgate Institute', *History Workshop Journal*, No.5, 1978, pp. 164–172; David Webb, *Bishopsgate Foundation Centenary History*, Published by the Governors of the Bishopsgate Foundation, 1991.
41 C.W.J. Harris, 'Charles Goss. Portrait of a Reactionary', *Library World*, July 1970.
42 C.W.J. Harris, *Charles William Frederick Goss (1864-1946)* (Unpublished thesis for a librarian qualification, n.d.).
43 *Clarion*, 4 January, 1896.
44 *Book and News Trade Gazette*, 23 November, 1895
45 See Raphael Samuel, 'No Mythic Golden Age', *New Statesman & Society*, 6 March 1992.
46 Bishopsgate Foundation, Report of the Governing Body, 1896.
47 Bishopsgate Foundation, Report of the Governing Body, 1898.
48 Bishopsgate Foundation, Report of the Governing Body, 1896–1914.
49 Bishopsgate Foundation and Institute, London, 1911.
50 Bishopsgate Foundation, Report of the Governing Body, 1896–1914.
51 Ibid.
52 Bishopsgate Foundation, Report of the Governing Body, 1903.
53 *Spectator*, 8 June, 1929.
54 Bishopsgate Institute Prospectus, Spring Term 2000; Bishopsgate Institute Prospectus, Autumn Term, 1999.
55 See n. 34 above.
56 Raphael Samuel, *A Testimonial in Support of Heritage Funds for the Bishopsgate Institute*, Unpublished paper, 31 January, 1996.
57 Ibid.

Sound judgements: the compact disc reissue scene as public history

Paul Martin

Going round in circles

A small American record company of the 1950s, Mar-Vel, optimistically boasted on its label that it was providing 'the hits of tomorrow recorded today'[1] while the 1990s reissue label, See For Miles, postmodernly advises us to: 'look forward to the past'.[2] Fifty years ago vinyl was a future orientated medium, whereas today's digital musical delivery often specialises in excavating vinyl history. It is the importance of older music reactivated by the compact disc (CD) that is the subject of this paper.

Musical taste is subjective and personalised, though its creative nature can reveal historical precedents to the seemingly innovative. Assumptions also tend to be made about the whole process of and engagement with record culture as a 'man thing' which women view as infantile. While record collecting is largely (though not exclusively) a male pursuit, as is the compilation of data and label issue reference material, the reissue scene is bigger than this and women are far from inactive in it. CD reissue in some ways challenges the perceived exclusivity of collecting, in that it compiles and makes generally available material which would otherwise be unobtainable. Media commentators have too readily dismissed retrospection as an easy substitute for a lack of future vision. We are fascinated with history in all forms as never before. This paper is in part an attempt to suggest the positiveness of this.[3] It would be easy to attribute the current interest in past music to a *fin de siècle* malaise, but the rediscovery of music is cyclical.[4] Reissues began with the long playing (LP) micro groove record (albeit with a narrower focus).[5] The CD is the latest and thus far the most efficient format for aural archiving, but with a far wider remit than before.

Older recordings in company archives are known as back catalogue. The most common of these in high street record shops are reissued 'classic albums' which range from Abba to ZZ Top. This represents the most commercial and lucrative end of the CD reissue market, produced mainly by major labels (EMI, Sony, etc.). Superficially, it panders to pure nostalgia, but *can* simultaneously serve as an entry point to a deeper exploration of older music.[6] This deeper aspect of the reissue market is that which concerns itself with the forgotten and unexplored recordings of the past, by obscure and little known artists, 'the foot soldiers of the rock and roll revolution'.[7] It is not Louis Jordan, Elvis Presley, The Beatles or Rolling Stones that concern us here, but rather the legions of wannabes that they inspired, adding texture, depth and richness to the linear gloss of media stardom. Both major and independent labels reissue old music, but the independent sector is the focus here, as it represents an art before profit principle in contradistinction to the ethos of the major labels. Indeed, master tapes may be leased from major labels by independents for limited reissue. In this way, old music is re-presented and heard as new, with a vibrancy that epitomises its cyclical value to us. The liner note writer of a recent box set of 1970s progressive music, for instance, noted that the music: 'somehow seems to be further away than the decade that preceded it'.[8] The CD reissue scene is busy reclaiming this as a lost archival legacy and restating it as history. I have focused on the 1960s for this paper, but the points made are as valid for other periods and musical genres.

Vinyl junkie or digipack fiend?
I do not wish to make an 'end of history' case for CD, as vinyl is where the reissue scene began and still in a limited way continues today. Therefore a look at the survival of vinyl in the digital age is integral to the understanding of cultural and technological shift and the resistance to it. With the invention of CD, we were assured that recording technology had

reached its zenith. The 1984 *Guinness Book of Recorded Sound*, when discussing the development of the CD noted: 'All these features have been brought to a level of technical perfection in the CD record beyond which it would seem impossible to progress...'[9] However, right from the beginning, there had been significant protest by vinylphiles at the corporate decision to drop vinyl in favour of the CD. Although vinyl manufacture declined in the 1980s, there remained, and indeed is growing, a significant preference for it, the CD being viewed as too clinical:

> ...figures from the British Phonographic Institute (BPI) for 1997 show that CD sales were down for the first time since the digital disc's launch in 1984, by 1.5 per cent. Vinyl, however, showed an increase of 7.7 per cent in sales for 1997 – the only format to do so – and turntable sales are up by 11 per cent.[10]

There is also a growing number of specialist providers of albums in audiophile vinyl[11] and secondary market shops dealing exclusively in vinyl. Here, vinyl is seen as 'real' or 'legitimate' history and is valued physically as an artefact, conceptually whole and untampered with by the addition of extra tracks or the remastering which CD employs.

Major record companies underestimated the significance of this un-nostalgic preference. Hip hop deejays could not spin or 'scratch' CD's, much of current dance culture is based on twelve-inch vinyl singles, and a considerable part of the market for roots reggae (of the 1970s) is in vinyl, because of the sonic dimensions that analogue sound provides for the bass and drums which underpin it. As one article noted:

> The shop [Peckings in London] only stocks authentic sound system tapes from the 70's, vinyl albums and singles. He [Chris Price, the shopow=ner] remains defiantly distrustful of CDs, complaining that on digitally remastered CDs "the bass is not heavy. If you've got loads of CDs it doesn't mean jack" he adds. "You're not seen as a connoisseur of music by holding CDs, as you are by holding records".[12]

There is also a low-fi sound, as personified by bands like Portishead, which incorporate sound samples of vinyl recordings on their CDs. They deliberately bring the surface crackles and pops into the foreground, as an aesthetic element, thus legitimising or valuing old technology in the context of the new. On the other hand, the CD has doubled the potential playing time of a disc (up to eighty minutes to the LP's forty).

For an increasing number, leisure listening has been transformed into a historical mission and material from past decades and musical genres is keenly sought. To service this sector, companies like Westside Records of London, license and reissue obscure blues, rockabilly and soul recordings which have languished unissued in personal and corporate basements for years. Marketing multiple CDs in boxed sets enables whole genres of music, rosters of labels or repertoires of artists to be acquired, surveyed, studied and heard holistically, often book-ended by historically relevant dates.[13] Sometimes included is the directional chatter between producer and artist in the studio or excerpts from old interviews.[14] They are included to give context to the work in progress and by interfering with the linear running of the music reaffirm the historical and documentary nature of the project. As such they constitute oral history. The inclusion of alternative versions or takes of some songs, originally unreleased, also affords us a broader understanding of musical style and conceptual development. In doing so, it enables us to see it in total as a historical process.

Archaeology – digging the scene

The nature of the research into and hunt for long forgotten master tapes and obscure records, has an archaeological quality about it. The assembling of disparate parts into a conceptual whole is almost forensic. A 1998 review of a four CD box set[15] looked at the regional pop music of mid 1960s America, arising in response to the 'British invasion' of beat groups. The box comprises some 118 tracks by various unknown and long defunct bands, expanding on the original 1972 double vinyl album which comprised 27 tracks (now CD 1 of the box). The reviewer, Ben Edmonds noted:

The story thrown in high relief by the expanded Nuggets is the disintegration of the regionalism that provided this music with its spiritual infrastructure. Most of these 45s were products of local scenes, each with a distinct indigenous flavour. That it wasn't just new York and L.A was precisely the point. It was Detroit and Minneapolis and the Pacific Northwest and San Jose, California, the entire state of Texas and even Keokuk, Iowa. Local flavour was a casualty of this music's success and the explosion of delivery technology; never again will we be this isolated from one another.[16]

Thus, these songs could be heard in a concise format in a way which they would never have been heard at the time of their original release. This is as true of Britain, if on a smaller scale, as of the USA. Differing music scenes in Belfast, Birmingham, Liverpool, London, Manchester or Newcastle were all much richer than the 'hit parade' of the 1960s reflects. It is the particular flavour of these scenes which CD reissue is especially interested in exposing for wider recognition.[17] In so doing, the reissue CD becomes a historical aural-geographical survey. On a national basis the productions of the legendary British producer Joe Meek, in the first half of the 1960s have been brought to prominence through extensive CD reissue programmes. Consequently, British musical sub-genres such as beat instrumentals have also found a new following through CD reissue, thus bringing about a historical re-evaluation of British pop music, of which 'Merseybeat' was only one flavour.[18] By extension 1960s beat and garage records from Australia, Europe (east and west), India, Latin America and elsewhere have also generated interest.[19] Thus the world impact of British beat and American rhythm and blues (r'n'b) of the 1960s can be more truly assessed and the music made available very widely.

These reissues also offer a holistic historical precedent for the communication of music on a global basis, three decades before the Internet enabled musicians to market their wares directly to the home. Firstly, then, digital recording technology does not necessarily mean the abandonment of what preceded it; secondly, where digital technology is employed, it is often as useful in reappraising our cultural past, as in promoting the novelty of the contemporary. Digital technology is used extensively for cleaning old studio tapes of extraneous sound, revealing old recordings to the listener as 'new'. Major record labels now run specialist subsidiaries or series devoted to the reissuing of long forgotten and now much in demand rarities from their vaults. Examples include *Polydor Chronicles* and *Warner Archives*. These old recordings have been marketed since the early 1990s as a historical legacy, whereas previously they were only seen as obsolete back catalogue. There are specialist music book services and shops, such as Cornwall's A&R Booksearch and London's Helter Skelter, while music magazines like *Mojo* and *Record Collector* should be seen as the public history journals of the high street magazine racks rather than transient leisure reading. Taken as part of this whole, the CD reissue scene disciplines the fascination with retrospective cultural identities and attitudes into public history.

The profusion of small independent record labels that sprung up after the Second World War in America alone was enormous and has left a vast legacy of undervalued recordings for reappraisal. As one Dutch reissuer of rock and roll records notes:

> Many [young rockers] have hardly seen ORIGINAL 45s from the 50s which sometimes results in questions like "You must have a big imagination to make up all those label names". They don't understand / believe that those records / labels really exist.[20]

Neither is the interest in older music and personal styles a cultural phenomenon only to be found at the end of the century. The Britain of the late 1950s for instance saw a collegiate taste for 1920s 'trad' jazz in contrast to the then current and working class preference for rock and roll. In the early 1960s Britain discovered the 'blues' of the 1940s and 1950s, while the northern soul scene of the 1970s, based on obscure uptempo soul records of the 1960s, is itself now the subject of revival in the 1990s.[21] Until recent years it could be argued, popular music has not been perceived as historical, but rather a serendipitous accumulation of fashion trends, entrepreneurially inspired fads and contrived nostalgia. Punk rock's (1976–78) mix and match approach to youth culture inspired a resurgence of rockabillies, skinheads, and a mod revival c.1979–81, along with young bands recreating 'authentic' music or merging modern styles with it.[22]

Since then there has been a renaissance in many musical forms, notably in blues and Latin music,[23] which the CD reissue market has serviced, not least by making records originally only released in other world territories available in Britain. Radio shows such as Mark Lamarr's *Shake Rattle & Roll*, on night time BBC Radio 2, and historical musical overviews such as the *All Singing, All Dancing* six part series on the history of northern soul,[24] have not only given that station a new hip image, but have contributed to the serious promotion of past music and its role as public history. These programmes have had as much to say on the history and anecdotal reportage of the labels, the industry and those who worked in it, as they have about the music itself.[25]

Cherchez la femme

One of the most significant outcomes of the CD reissue scene has been the revelation of a hidden (or ignored) aspect of women's history. Images of women in 1960s popular music include the female pop or soul diva, solo or fronting a male band, the girl group vocal trio or the singer-songwriter (with piano or guitar). However, the all-girl rock band, playing their own instruments was a rarity and their output even more so.[26] Two important CDs, by She and The Luv'd Ones,[27] both American bands exemplify this.[28] In She's case, only one single was ever released, although they recorded enough material between 1965 and 1970 to compile a one-hour CD. The Luv'd Ones recorded several singles for independent labels between 1964 and 1966, but hours of home and studio demo recordings later surfaced and their founder, Char(lotte) Vinnedge was interviewed about the band shortly before her death in 1998.[29] The music of this period has been researched on a local basis.[30] In so doing, there have been discoveries of under-recorded female rock bands who were seen at best as a novelty by record companies. Indeed, Wildwood Records for whom The Tremolons (later The Luv'd Ones) recorded two singles in 1964, printed on the record label 'All Girl Combo'.[31] They did, however, compete with each other in battles of the bands and also with male groups in 'battles of the sexes'.[32]

Given the male-dominated rock scene, however, girls who wanted to make the transition from fan to musician were strongly inhibited from doing so, and the courage required to break free of gender and peer conventions must have been considerable at that time. Char Vinnedge recalls the reluctance of female musicians to form a group with her, while the band She recounted a gig when, as their guitarist Janis Volkoff launched into a lead solo, a male voice from the crowd shouted: 'girls can't do that!'.[33] Although in common with male garage bands, their content was largely non-political, the very existence of these female bands was a political statement in itself. Another American female teen band The Exotics did however change their name in 1965 to The Nineteenth Amendment (for female enfranchisement): '...to signify they wanted equal treatment as women.'[34] There remains much more to be researched in this area. Little is known about many of the members of the groups and how they were affected by their musical experiences.[35] The CD reissue scene has at least brought this to wider public attention. It is though not just female rock bands that have been denied recognition.

It's here in black and white
When Bob Marley recorded *Punky Reggae Party* in 1977, it was in recognition of punk's affinity with roots reggae as a form of street-wise protest music.[36] However, it had been a similar adoption of early dance hall reggae by another white working class subculture, skinheads, in the late 1960s that had given reggae its impetus outside the Afro-Caribbean community. The white rock establishment rubbished reggae when it was first played, but skinheads adopted it as their own and has become known as skinhead reggae in Britain because of this.[37] Reggae artists indeed recorded tributes to the fact.[38] This seems to contradict the popular image of skinheads as racist thugs. Of course, many unfortunately are, but the international organisation, SHARP (Skinheads Against Racial Prejudice) is also important. Not all skinheads are white and there have been socialist and anti-racist skinhead bands such as The Redskins, while skinhead style has long since been adopted by gay men and women. There is also a Trojan Records skinhead club.[39] The picture is thus more complicated than we might casually assume, as the early reggae reissues remind us.

Reggae pioneers such as Laural Aitkin and Dandy Livingstone, who lived, worked, recorded and produced reggae in Britain are still largely unheralded outside fan circles. Prince Buster and Desmond Dekker were the Jamaican kings of reggae in the 1960s and had cult followings of mods and skinheads in Britain.[40] Aitkin, whose *Boogie In My Bones* single from 1959, is often credited with being the first ska record, and who was one of the first to record a reggae record, has lived mostly in England since the 1960s,[41] but it is only through the reissuing of some of his Pama and Trojan label recordings from the 1960s that his importance has begun to be recognised. In Bristol, it was only in 1999 that there was any public recognition that the city's wealth was born out of the slave trade.[42] In contrast the CD reissue scene has been vital in promoting the importance of black presence in modern Britain by keeping reggaes' British dimension in the public domain. In so doing, significant cultural and public history is being reclaimed for black and white alike.

What is still missing in large part is the oral and ephemeral history of how music was consumed by British Afro-Caribbeans in the 1950s and 1960s. There are clues in earlier historically hidden figures like the Trinidadian guitarist Lauderic Caton, who pioneered the use of the electric guitar in Britain as early as 1940, playing in small jazz bands in numerous black London clubs at that time.[43] Which were the specialist record shops? Where were the clubs that catered for Afro-Caribbean music?[44] What was the first exposure to such music like for young black Britons in these years? How was this perceived in respect to white pop and rock which was dominant on the radio, and so on? There is therefore a great deal of scope for oral history to reveal the process of engagement with music by British Afro-Caribbeans. The reissue scene at least attempts to rehabilitate some of those who produced it. It has also brought to light other little known areas of black musical history, such as *From Where I Stand: the black experience of country music*, a three CD box set (Warner Nashville) which explores the black dimensions of a predominantly white music.[45]

Better the second time round – the reissue labels

Much of the reappraisal of older music has been promoted by individual fans who have started their own labels for the purpose of reissuing their favourite music which they feel has been neglected or uncatered for. These small reissue labels are often run by one person or couples and partners, who reissue discs from a sense of commitment to and passion for the period music of their choice. This missionary zeal is often communicated through personal declarations of purpose and motivation in liner notes, and which demonstrate the narrow margin between historical passion and financial solvency. One such label is Bear Family in Hamburg, run by its founder Richard Weize. Weize epitomises the independent reissue company ethos and is therefore worth quoting at some length from an interview with him in 1995:[46]

Q. Does Bear Family make money on the boxed sets?

A. Sometimes yes, sometimes not, but that is not the point. Bear Family records is probably my vision of reissuing music as it should be done. First creating a good product and then trying to sell it. We are fortunate enough to have a successful mail order operation that can subsidise the issues. I am not into money, as long as I am able to make a living. It comes down to the fact that if I won a million dollars in the lottery, I would only issue more records. As far as I am concerned, the music and artists must not be forgotten. The problem however, is that sales between 1000 and 2000 copies don't pay for the expensive production costs.

Q. The sound of your CDs is considered to be the best, your booklets are amongst the most extensive with many rare pictures. How do you do this?

A. The reasons I suppose are many. First we are licensing the masters from the copyright holders and do not take advantage of the copyright laws that enable old masters to be issued without payment after a certain number of years. This enables me to have access to the best possible tape copies. With the help of archivists at the labels I do a lot of research to make sure that we get the first generation tapes, or the best possible alternative. I am in the studio while the tapes are copied digitally. This is time consuming but important. The advantage we have in comparison with other companies is due to the fact that we are not commercially orientated. We can postpone a release until we are satisfied with the quality. Some of the projects have been put on the backburner for up to seven years. The next step is that we use the best possible mastering engineers, who understand the music and bring their own skill and knowledge. Another reason for our reputation is that we recreate the old sound – not like others who change it. We are not producers, we are reissue producers at most. The original engineers, producers, knew exactly what they were doing. We have to honour that.

As far as I am concerned, I just want to keep history alive, to make sure that the music is not forgotten. People had visions at the time, which need to be kept alive. It is my vision to be part of it. Anyway, we then try to get the most knowledgeable writers and researchers for the project. We usually try to work with the artist, his family and relatives. We try to locate unpublished and rare photos, and try to use first generation prints. We research the discography as much as possible. We take special pride in our boxed sets. Many are complete career retrospectives while others are complete within certain time periods. We always package them in the LP sized box so that the text is easily readable and the impact of the photos isn't lost.

Q. How do you decide what you will issue?

A. This really depends. I suppose I have no detailed plan. Every project that makes sense. We have issued material as diverse as country blues, rhythm and blues and jazz. ... We also take pride in the fact that we will issue a boxed set by historically significant artists with little or no commercial potential like Jimmie Driftwood, Tommy Collins, Johnny and Jack, Marvin Rainwater and Johnny Western.

The motivation for other reissue label owners is born out of a sense of resentment at the neglect accorded to the music they love. Two labels reissuing Australian 1960s beat and garage music exemplify this:

> I'm the first to admit that our music was not all great...or even good. However, the percentage of our really bad music was no greater that what came into this country from overseas. Our problem stemmed from the fact that we were never a trend setter but the followers of overseas trends. And the reason for this was solely our population and not the quality of the music. I started Canetoad Records in early 1987. The sole aim was to reissue some of the music with the respect that it deserved.[47]

> So little seems to be known of the hundreds of non-hit Australian recording acts of the 60s – both in and out of the country. Our damned national inferiority complex led us to believe that it was all derivative fluff...[48]

The motivation can also be simply an evangelical urge to share the good news of music which has affected the owner of the label:

> We both have the same amount of absolute passion for music and when we find records, we want to share it with every other like minded person and get other people to share their music too. It's too cool to be unavailable to hear. One piece of music can change or sincerely affect another person's life or musical taste on the other side of the globe, or on the other hand down the road![49]

Emphasis is often placed either on the quality of the sources and technology used in digital transfer, or the lack of them. In the 1980s 'classic' reissue compilers for the major labels were almost apologising for the 'dated' sound of the music:

> It would be dangerous to suggest that these 20 year-old recordings don't sound dated – the passing of time is an impossible opponent – but that they remain classics of a great era cannot be denied.[50]

In the 1990s, though, independent compilers were positively revelling in it:

> These tracks were compiled from singles, and dusty forgotten tapes and acetates. There is noise, clicking, dropout and hum – these you must endure to experience the godlike R+B power of the Chants.[51]

> Note: This is primitive, raw R&R! As the master tapes have vanished, these CDs are re-mastered from the cleanest available copies. Some surface noise does turn up -- but baby, that is R&R.[52]

Some independent reissue labels equate the 'raw' sounds of the teen bands of the 1950s and 1960s, including the primitive sound quality of much of it, with 'authenticity'. This is often juxtaposed against the perceived sterility of contemporary music. There is then a sense of mission and subversion[53] of historical obligation to make the more obscure recordings of these earlier decades accessible and to spread the message of their importance.

Reading music
Quite apart from being aural documents, reissue CDs when supplied with good liner notes in the accompanying booklets also become written chronicles or historical tracts in their own right.[54] Liner notes cover a number of topics: biographical and musicological information about the artists; history of the labels on which they recorded; essays on the development of the music concerned or recording facilities, sometimes incorporating footnotes and reference sources for further reading; rare photographs and/or reproductions of trade advertisements for the original records. They provide a history often more detailed than can be found in reference books.[55] Many of those commissioned to write them are chosen because of their reputation for knowledge in the area, with numerous magazine articles or books on the subject to their credit.[56] Reissue labels frequently provide additional information on websites, or newsletters such as Ace Records' *Get on the Right Track*, which not only serves as an advert for their latest reissues, but also includes additional historical information on them. Catalogues and lists themselves, available free or at minimal charge from the labels, can be read as public history browsers as well as reference sources.

Additionally, the half-century legacy of 'rock'n'roll' has in recent years seen a great burgeoning of accessible literature which expands on the themes addressed in liner notes.[57] This is quite separate from the more academic literature which has grown in the same period. Fanzines devoted to period music, subcultures and so on have also flourished as never before[58] and reissue label owners have become archivists:

> ...*New England Teen Scene* was a magazine back in the mid-60s and surviving copies provide us with a glimpse into the local New England rock scene back then. In fact it was one of the very first magazines to document the local scene...New England had a fertile scene back in the sixties

and hundreds of 45's and LP's that were released document the bands and the times.[59]

And to close the show for us this evening...

The CD reissue scene enables us to understand the randomness of stardom, how but for a quirk of fate a completely obscure artist would have had the hit record that allowed someone else to enhance an international reputation.[60] Independent reissuers provide platforms for neglected artists to be heard again, perhaps for the first time in decades and to be heard both with new historical insight into the creative process and as a contextual dimension for careers of more familiar names.[61] This enables the familiar international hit record to be sited in a much wider context and heard as part of a bigger picture, rather than as a predestined 'rock classic',[62] which radio especially has conditioned us to, abbreviating history to nostalgia. The popular interest in the history and running of record labels, especially the myriad independent labels that sprung up after the Second World War[63] and which have been reissued on CD, affords deeper insight into the hit or miss business of searching for artists and promoting records in an era before it became an overwhelmingly corporatised and sanitised process.

The proliferation of television programmes and series such as the BBC's Dancing In The Street, Rock Family Trees or Channel Four's Mr Rock and Roll (profiling managers) and The Hip-Hop Years (on the rise of rap music), recognise the interest in the historical nature of post-war youth culture. Such programmes, in conjunction with the media already discussed, act as a kind of informal musical open university.[64] In this way, people become intellectually primed for history, even without recognising it.

The computer age now offers even wider choice in this process. Like CD, once the more obvious and lucrative 'classic album' market becomes saturated, more overlooked work will become available to be downloaded onto portable hard drives, or compiled from one's own choice over the Net onto bespoke CDs. The release of new music on the Net both exclusively and as a promotional taster, already challenges the traditional record industry. How this will alter the shape of musical production, distribution and consumption overall remains to be seen. What remains certain is that there is infinitely more music from the past yet to be rediscovered and reissued.[65] The technology of the future will no doubt continue to aid the resurrection of neglected music of the past. It is younger people who are the most enthusiastic about this music, for whom the archaeological and research aspects of the reissue process are a real engagement with twentieth-century history. It was only in the 1980s that tabloid newspapers were decrying the Rolling Stones for still performing 'at their age'. By the 1990s young tribute bands were performing and imitating the songs of those from the 1960s and 1970s.[66] Older styles of music from half a century ago have been revived by young musicians[67] and everyone who played in a 1960s band seems to have done a reunion tour.[68] In our post-industrial age where the rules or boundaries by which society was kept compartmentalised have dissolved, age is not the barrier it once was. The last word however, might usefully be left to Wayne Proctor, a one-time member of American garage band, We The People, whose recent double CD retrospective was highly praised by critics.[69] I will leave it as a disputed point for further discussion as to whether it is 'healthier' for the tastes of age and youth to be harmonised or to remain oppositional:

...the 'fun' music of the '60s has crossed over the boundaries of the so-called generation gap, and will never leave us. You like it and I like it. Because of this music, my children and I have the same likes and dislikes. That never happened with me and my parents. How will it be when you have children?[70]

Appendix
Sources for 1950s and 1960s reissues

The following labels deal in reissued popular music. The list is far from exhaustive. Subscription to specific fanzines (advertised in (e.g.) *Mojo* magazine) will reveal further genre-specific labels.

Ace Records,(including Big Beat) 42–50 Steele Road, London, NW10 7AS
A&R Booksearch, High Close, Winnick Cross, Lanreath, Looe, Cornwall, PL13 2PF
Arf! Arf! Records, PO Box 465, Middleborough, MA 02346, USA
Bear Family Records, PO Box 1154, D-27727 Hamburg, Germany
Bomp / AIP, PO Box 7112, Burbank, California, CA 91510
Collector Records & CDs, PO Box 1200, Oud Beyerland, 3260 AE, Netherlands.
Crypt, PO. Box 304292, D-20325 Hamburg, Germany
Diamond Recordings, Heckfield Place, 530 Fulham Road, London, SW6 5NR
Finbarr International, Folkstone, Kent CT20 2QQ

Helter Skelter Books, 4 Denmark Street, London, WC2H 8LL
Magpie Direct Music, PO Box 25, Ashford, Middlesex, TW15 1XL
Norton Records, PO Box 646 Cooper Station, New York, NY10276, USA
Red Lick, Porthmadog, Gwynedd, Wales, LL49 9DJ.
Rhino, 10635 Santa Monica Blvd., Los Angeles, California CA 90025-4900, USA
See For Miles, PO Box 328, Maidenhead, Berkshire, SL6 2NE
Sequel, A29 Barwell Business Park, Leatherhead Road, Chessington, Surrey
Specialist Record Services, Regent House, 1 Pratt Mews, London, NW1 0AD
Sundazed Music Inc., PO Box 85, Coxsackie, New York, NY12051, USA
Westside, West Heath Yard, 174 Mill Lane, London, NW6 1TB

Notes

1. T. Abramson – 'Vive la Revolution', *Guardian*, The Guide, 9/01/1999 front cover.
2. On marketing and promotional materials such as Tee shirts and catalogues
3. I wish to thank the Ruskin public history discussion group for raising these as points of contention. For gender differences in collecting practice see the following: R. Belk and M. Wallendorf, 'Of Mice and Men: gender identity in collecting', republished in S.Pearce (ed.), *Interpreting Objects and Collections*, Routledge, London, 1994, pp. 240–253; S. Pearce, *On Collecting*, Routledge,London, 1995, pp. 197–222; P. Martin, *Popular Collecting and the Everyday Self: the reinvention of museums?*, Cassell, London,1999, pp. 67–98.
4. See R. Kennedy & R. McNutt. *Little Labels – Big Sound: small record companies and the rise of American music*, University of Indiana Press, Bloomington, 1999.
5. For a full history of record development see A. Millard, *America On Record: a history of recorded sound*, Cambridge University Press, Cambridge, 1995; E. Kohler, *Vintage Record Graphics 1940–1960*, Chronicle Books, San Francisco, 1999 and the *American Collectors' Journal 78 Quarterly* for early history (available from Red Lick Records, see Appendix).
6. T.V. series such as Carlton's Classic Albums (1999) and the BBC's Top Of The Pops 2 (a reprise of vintage TOTP appearances) also make this visual.
7. Rockin' From Coast to Coast Vol.1 CD, Ace Records catalogue 1998, p. 49. British examples include: The Beat Scene, The R'n'B Scene, The Mod Scene, The Freakbeat Scene CDs on Decca / EMI.
8. 'J.I' quoting David Wells in reviewing A Dawn Anthology, *Mojo* No.73, December 1999, p. 128.
9. R. Dearling, C. Dearling, B. Rust, *The Guinness Book of Recorded Sound*, Guinness Superlatives, London, 1984, p. 212.
10. T. Cox, 'Full Circle', *Guardian*, 20/10/1998, p. 4. Turntables are now also available for adding to'mini-hi fi' systems e.g. Innovations catalogue, June 1999. Mark Lamarr's Vinyl Maniacs, BBC Radio 2, 16/10/1999, also investigated the attraction of vinyl in the digital age.
11. i.e. heavy, virgin vinyl for best possible audio sound reproduction, which was originally used primarily for classical music recordings.
12. J. Maycock, 'Big Noise in the Bush', Peckings, Shepherds Bush, London, *Mojo*, No.53, April 1998, p. 127. See also p. Martin 'Look, See, Hear: a remembrance with approaches to contemporary public history at Ruskin' in G. Andrews, H. Kean, J. Thompson, (eds.) *Ruskin College: Contesting Knowledge, Dissenting Politics*, Lawrence & Wishart, London, 1999, pp. 155–159

13 e.g. Duke Ellington Centennial Edition: The Complete RCA Victor Recordings1927-1973, a twenty-four CD box set. See review by C. Ingham – 'A Wild Nobility', *Mojo*, No.68, July 1999, pp. 88–90; Various – The Voice of the People, a twenty CD series documenting British folk music. See review by C. Greig 'The archaic and the arcane', *Mojo*, No.62, January 1999, pp. 92–94.
14 Interestingly on the double CD anthology Sam Cooke's SAR, Records Story 1959–1965, (Abkco) and The Zombies 'Live At the BBC', disc four of Zombie Heaven, four CD box set (Big Beat). Such inclusions can also illustrate the breakdown of working relationships as on Various Artists – Someone To Love: the birth of the San Francisco sound CD, (Big Beat): 'Included here are false starts and studio chat to illustrate the animosity between band and producer...' previewed in *Get On the Right Track*, No.21, Oct.1996.
15 Nuggets: original artefacts from the first psychedelic era 1965-1968, Rhino Records, four CD box set, USA import
16 B. Edmonds, 'There Goes the Neighbourhood', *Mojo*, No.58, September 1998, pp. 92–93.
17 See for example the Belfast Beat Maritime Blues (Big Beat) and Brumbeat CDs. Also: S. Cohen, *Rock Culture in Liverpool*, Clarendon Press, London, 1991; A. Clayson, *Beat Merchants*, Blandford Press, London, 1995; A. Clayson, *Hamburg – The Cradle of British Rock*, Sanctuary Publishing, London, 1997; A. Lawson, *It Happened in Manchester*, International Music Publications, 1998
18 For the Joe Meek story see J. Repsch, *The Legendary Joe Meek, the Telstar Man*, Woodford House, London, 1989; for CDs with his and other early 1960s British pop recordings see 'Diamond Recordings' in the Appendix. For further reference to British pre-Beatles pop, see S. Leigh & J. Firminger, *Half Way To Paradise: Britpop1955–1962*, Finbarr International Publications, Kent, 1996; D. McAleer, *Hit Parade Heroes: British Beat Before the Beatles*, Hamlyn, London, 1993; Various Artists, British Beat Before the Beatles 1955–1962 (EMI) CDs in 6 volumes.
19 e.g.: Various Artists CDs: Exitos A Go Go: teenbeat south of the border (Latin America) (AIP); Planetary Pebbles Vol.1 (Eastern Europe) (AIP); Pebbles Vol.12 -The World (AIP) (Austria, France, Holland, Italy, Japan, Lebanon etc.) etc.; Ugly Things . (Australia, Raven); Girls in the Garage: Asian Babes (two volumes) (Romulan); GS I Love You: Japanese Garage Bands of the 1960s (Big Beat)
20 C. Klop, 30 years of Collector Records 1967–1997, catalogue introduction
21 R. Pruter, *Chicago Soul*, University of Illinois Press, Chicago, 1992; D.Nowell, *Too Darn Soulful: the story of northern soul*, Robson Books, London, 1999.
22 Such as the Coventry based 'Two-Tone' ska label in 1979, noveau rockabilly and a 1960s garage rock revival, for which see T. Gassen, *Knights of Fuzz: The Garage and Psychedelic Music Explosion 1980-1995*, Borderline Productions, Glasgow, 1997
23 e.g. the phenomenal rise to fame of the Afro-Cuban All Stars, featuring a number of octogenarian singers and musicians
24 Other recent examples of Radio 2 historical profiles include: The Stax Records Story, May 1998; Berry Gordy's Motown (records) Feb–March 1999; Jerry Wexler Soul Man (producer for Atlantic Records), July–August 1999.
25 See Appendix of reissue labels whose CD liner notes exemplify this.
26 A Czech band, The Olympics, recorded an ode to such female musicians c.1965; The Story Of The Girl With The Bass Guitar (Sufbeat Behind The Iron Curtain Part 2. AIP CD 1999). For a post 1970 study see, M. Bayton, *Frock Rock: women performing popular music*, Oxford University Press, 1998.

Bayton's is perhaps the only book thus far to focus on the experience of women as contemporary rock musicians on a parochial level rather than on rock stars.

27 She – She Wants A Piece Of You, (Big Beat, UK); The Luv'd Ones – Truth's Gotta Stand, (Sundazed, USA). See also the Girls in the Garage series of LPs and CDs on Romulan (USA).
28 For a British example see 'The Beat Chics' from Liverpool on Deram/EMI CD The Beat Scene for their only record 'Now I Know' from 1964. They also played the tough German club circuit.
29 The results of which appeared as the liner notes.
30 Published in fanzines, often advertised in *Mojo* and *Record Collector* magazines, available in WH Smith.
31 Pictured on the reissue sleeve of their extended play single in 1996 (Sundazed)
32 e.g. see J. Oldsberg, *The Flip Side: an illustrated history of southern Minnesota rock & roll music from 1955-1970*, self published, second edition, Minnesota USA, 1997. Examples include chapters on female garage bands The Exotics, Continental Co-ets and the Silver Shadows.
33 Both cases are recalled in the liner notes to The Luv'd Ones and She CDs.
34 Oldsberg, *The Flip Side*, p. 79
35 Although in some cases, there is more oral history than recorded legacy, see examples cited in note 32.
36 See e.g. D. Widgery, *Beating Time: Riot 'n' Race 'n' Rock 'n' Roll*, London, Chatto & Windus, 1986.
37 See M. Griffiths, *Boss Sounds: classic skinhead reggae*, Argyll, Skinhead Times Publishing, 1995.
38 See Trojan CDs: Skinhead Revolt and Symarip Skinhead Moonstomp. The skinhead reggae sound is also exemplified on Lee Perry-The Complete UK Uppsetter Singles, Vol.1,1969, and Tighten Up Vols. 1 & 2.
39 Trojan, along with Pama was the first record label to release reggae music in Britain, (Chris Blackwell's Island and Emil Shallit's Blue Beat labels had previously introduced ska to Britain) and which in recent years has undertaken a comprehensive CD reissue programme of early reggae music. The Pama catalogue still remains largely unreissued. See also S. Barrow and P. Dalton, *Reggae – The Rough Guide*, Rough Guides Ltd., London, pp. 325–329 for a synoptic overview of reggae's early development in Britain and Griffiths, *Boss Sounds* for a detailed study of record labels.
40 Prince Buster recently saw the reissue of his 1966 Whine and Grine record, used in a Levis advert, making the charts in 1998. See also Lloyd Bradley, 'One Step Beyond' (the Prince Buster story), *Mojo*, No.46, September 1997, pp. 44–50; Various Artists CD, Reggae In Your Jeggae: British reggae 1968–1972 (Trojan); Laural Aitkin – The Pama Years, (Grover, Germany).
41 For biographical sketches of both Aitkin and Livingstone see Griffiths, *Boss Sounds,* pp. 33–34; 35–37; C. Larkin ed., *The Guinness Who's Who of Reggae*, Middlesex, Guinness Publishing, 1994, pp. 8–10; 153–154
42 Untold: The Slave Trade, Programme 1, Channel Four, 3rd October 1999
43 V. Wilmer, 'I've Created A Monster!', *Mojo*, No.44, July 1997: 25-27; V. Wilmer, 'Lauderic Caton electric guitar pioneer', obituary, *Mojo*, No.65, April, 1999, p. 32.
44 See Maycock, 'Big Noise in the Bush' for example of a specialist shop in the 1960s; Grifiths, *Boss Sounds* reproduces adverts of some clubs and stockists.
45 See M. Hagen's review in *Mojo*, No.56, July 1998, p. 99.
46 Interview with R. Weize by W. Fuchs in *20 Years of Bear Family Records 1975-1995*, Hamburg 1995, pp. 13–15.

47 D. Mittlehauser, notes to The Australian Music Beat Scene (1965-67) The Go!! / Scope labels CD, n/d
48 1980 liner notes to vinyl volume of Various Artists – Ugly Things, reissued on CD in 1992 on Raven (Australia).
49 M. Mills 'All Aboard the Acid Machine', *Shindig*, No.3, n/d p. 45. Interview with the two owners of 'Dig The Fuzz' reissue record label.
50 J. Tobler liner notes to The Animals – Singles Plus, CD, EMI 1987.
51 Liner note to Chants R&B – Stagedoor Witchdoctors CD on Zero Records of New Zealand.
52 Back of jewel case to Back From The Grave Part Three on German Crypt Label. (1964–67 recordings).
53 For example, it is not the Motown hit records of the 1960s that are most in demand, but those that flopped or were covered by other Motown artists but not released etc. See This Is Northern Soul: 24 Tamla Motown Rarities (Debutante, 2 volumes)
54 e.g. Rob Bowman, a music professor, wrote the liner notes for three large box sets on the history of Stax Records (one of the three main 1960s soul labels along with Atlantic and Tamla Motown). He won the 1996 Grammy 'Best Album Notes' category for his 47,000 word monograph that accompanied the ten-CD box set., The Complete Stax / Volt Soul Singles Volume 3: 1972–1975. See R. Bowman, *Soulsville USA: the Story of Stax Records*, Books With Attitude, London, 1997.
55 Although the smallness of the print can sometimes be a strain to read, it is usually worth the perseverance!
56 e.g. Peter Grendysa – Over 400 of his articles, reviews and columns have appeared in music magazines and he has contributed booklet essays for more than 100 albums and CDs. Cited in *20 Years Bear Family Records 1975–1995*, p. 21.
57 Most of which can be found in the catalogues of A&R Booksearch and Helter Skelter Books (see Appendix)
58 Whilst acknowledging the 1960s underground, notably *Oz* and later *Punk* as the most well known improvisers of fanzines, they were all linear, i.e. about the times in which they were published; of the enormous number of fanzines now available, many are retrospective / historical.
59 E. Lindgren, liner notes to New England Teen Scene CD (Arf! Arf!) USA 1994.
60 e.g. Smiley Lewis who failed to make an impression with 'Blue Monday', which was later a hit for Fats Domino, 'One Night', which slightly amended was a hit for Elvis Presley or 'I Hear You Knocking', which was a hit in 1970 for Dave Edmunds. See Smiley Lewis, Shame, Shame, Shame, a four CD box set on Bear Family Records.
61 See e.g. West Texas Bop CD (Ace) featuring 1957-59 recordings by little known contemporaries of Buddy Holly, Holly himself plays guitar on some of them. The CD contextualises him as only the most famous exponent of a wider regional sound.
62 e.g. Little Richard in the context of the rest of the Specialty Records roster. See The Specialty Box (five CDs) on Ace Records; Art Rupe – In His Own Words: the Specialty Records Story, (two spoken word/ music Cds) (Ace). Rupe's Specialty label recorded Little Richard in the 1950s.
63 See e.g. Kennedy & McNutt. Little Labels; J. Picardie & D. Wade, *Atlantic and the Godfathers of Rock and Roll*, Fourth Estate, London,1993; A. Shaw, *Honkers and Shouters: the golden years of rhythm and blues*, MacMillan, New York, 1978.

64 H. Purcell, 'Broadcast History', *History Today*, Vol. 49 (11) November 1999, pp. 40-42 gives a detailed overview of history on television and its popularity.
65 This though, is not to argue that everything rediscovered is worth reissuing!
66 e.g. Bjorn Again (Abba) ReGenesis (Genesis); The Australian Doors; The Counterfeit Stones; Bootleg Beatles etc.
67 The jive / r'n'b scene of the 1940s for one, e.g. Brian Setzner Orchestra – The Dirty Boogie CD (Interscope) 1997; Sugar Ray's Flying Fortress – Bim Bam Baby (Ace) CD 1998.
68 These vary from 'cult bands' such as The Pretty Things, The Troggs and The Zombies to any number of reformed 1960s beat bands playing the holiday camp and chicken-in-a basket cabaret circuit.
69 The Mirror of Our Minds (Sundazed CD, USA).
70 M. Mills, 'In The Past: an interview with Wayne Proctor of We The People', *Shindig*, No.3 n/d: 18-21, p. 21. This paper is intended as recognition of the legacy that young musicians now have to draw upon, and which has already proven through various influences, to have enriched the creative process rather than hindered it. See Martin, 'Look See Hear', p. 156.

Index

Absence
  and gender issues, 16
  women and the sea 81–103
  in maritime museum exhibits 81–103
  of family issues, 141
Ace Records (UK), 182
Actresses' Franchise League, 42
Acts of Parliament
  Ancient Monuments Protection Act 1900, 71
  Ancient Monuments Act 1931, 71
  Cheap Trains Act 1864, 112
  Destructive Imported Animals Act 193, 64 n61
  Metropolitan Building Act 1854, 116
  National Heritage Act 1980, 52
  National Trust Act 1907, 71
  Pests Act 1954, 59
Adams, W.E., 163
Addison, Dr., 58
Ailesbury, Marquess of, 75
Aitkin, Laural, 178
Anne of the Indies (film), 88
Applegarth, Robert, 163
A&R Booksearch, 175, 184
Aubrey, John, 67, 72, 76
Austen, Jane, 128–129
Australian National Maritime Museum, 84, 90, 98
Avebury In Danger, 67, 75
Avebury Manor, 75
Bachelard, Gaston, 20
Back catalogue, 172
Backteller(s) and Backtelling, 39, 40
Baden-Powell, Lord, 32
Baldwin, Stanley, 55
Banford Library, 154
Bank of England 158
Barthes, Roland, 21, 24, 33
  and punctum, 21, 22, 28, 33
  and studium, 21, 23, 25, 29, 33
Bazalgette, Joseph, 116
Bear Family Records, 179–180, 184
Beatles, The, 172
Bedford, Duke of, 28, 54
Belloc, Hilaire, 166
Bennett, Tony, 39
Berger, John, 30
Betjeman, John, 74
Birmingham Council House, 144
Birmingham Library Service, 133
Birmingham Museum and Art Gallery, 127, 144
  and Birmingham History Gallery, 145
  and Gallery, 33, 144
Birmingham Royal Ballet, 130
Bishopsgate Club, The, 157

Bishopsgate Foundation, The, 167
Bishopsgate Ward Club, The, 157
Bishopsgate Ratepayers Association, The, 157
Black Country Society, 137
Blair, Eric, *see* Orwell, George,
Bowes-Lyon, Elizabeth, *see* Queen Mother
Boundaries 151–170
  blurring of, 15,
  and class, 114
  dissolution of, 184
  geographical, 76, 105–122, 152
Bourdieu, Pierre, 83
Bradlaugh, Charles, 151
Brennan, Barbara (née Jewson), 45
British Association for Local History, 45
British Field Sports Association, 56
British Records Association, 45
Bryce, Professor, 161
Brewin, Alan, 132
Brewin Books, 132
British Workers Sports Federation, 56
Broeze, Frank, 96
Browning, Mrs. B., 143
Builder, The, 116
Burgin, Victor, 22
Buster, Prince, 178
Butcher, Helen, 141
Campbell, Lady Colin, 32
Canetoad Records, 181
Cannadine, David, 13
Canning, George, 118
Carlova, John, 98
Caton, Lauderic, 179
Centreprise Books, 139
Charities, Parochial, 152, 153, 156
Charles, Prince, 137
Chas 'n' Dave, 135
Chinn, Dr Carl, 133–148
Citizenship, 157, 158
City of London College, 156
City of London Corporation, 158–159
  and new library 1873, 159
  and museum in Basinghall Street, 159
City Press, The, 161
Clarion Guild of Handcraft Exhibition, 161
Clarke, Roy, 133
Classic albums, 172, 183
Cobden Club, 157
Collecting and collections, 45, 46, 90, 159, 167
Collins, Tommy, 180
Commonwealth War Graves Commission, 44
Community, 71, 72, 77, 82, 96, 106, 112, 114, 133, 138, 142, 152, 155, 167
Cook, Captain, 88
Le Corbusier,136

Country Life, 52, 55, 57
Cox, Nicola, 137
Crane, Walter, 159
Crooks, Will, 161
Crow, Alan, 141
Dayus, Kathleen, 140, 141
Dekker, Desmond, 178
Deleuze, Giles, 100
Derrida, Jaques, 100
Diary (ies), 15, 37–50, 91
Doolan, Ed, 127
D'Oyly Carte Opera Company, 130
Douglas, Alton, 132, 134
Driftwood, Jimmie, 180
Druett, Joan, 98
Du Maurier, Daphne, 28, 30, 31
Dunwich Museum, 61
Dyos, H.J., 113
Edmunds, Ben, 174
Edward IV, 31
Edwards, Tracy, 88
Ehrenzweig, Anton, 33
Elder Dempster (shipping) Line, Merseyside, 81
E.M.I., 172
Empire Marketing Board, 57
English Heritage, 14, 61, 65–79, 119
Englishness
  construction of ideas of, 56, 128
  views of, 56, 58, 142, 143
  decline in quality of, 142
  Symbols of, 15, 52
  unEnglishness, 130
Enloe, Cynthia, 87
Evening Mail (Birmingham) 127, 129, 133, 134, 142, 143
Exclusion
  of women, 83, 90, 91, 98
  historical practice, 16
  stories, 145
Exotics, The (band), 177
Fabian Society, 157
Family History, 37–50
  Fair, 1998, 44
  magazine, 49
Family Records Centre, 43, 44, 45, 49
Fanzines, 182
Federation of Family History Societies, 45
Ferrier, Kathleen, 32
The Field, 52, 55, 57, 58, 59
Flayhart III, Henry William, 87
Fodie, Captain Sally, 82
Foretelling, 39, 42
Fortune, John, 65
Fox Talbot, 24
Freedom Press, The, 151
Free Libraries, 159, 164
Friends of The Public Record Office, 45
Fry, Katherine, 109, 122
Gas, Light and Coke Company, London, 116, 118
Gender
  awareness, 83, 88, 97
  balance, 82
  binary image, 85
  and collecting 185n3
  conventions, 177
  differences, 82
  in museum exhibits, 90
  issues, 88
  relations, 94, 98
  and the sea, 100

politics, 42, 152
Genealogical Society, 45
Genealogy, 37–50
General Strike 1926, 89
Gentlemen's Magazine, 165
Get On The Right Track, 182
Giffard, Ann, 98
Globalisation, 129
Gorman, John, 109, 112, 119, 122
Gormley, Anthony, 130
Goss, Charles William Frederick, 162, 164–165, 166
Goss-Custard, Reginald, 166
Greenaway, Councillor, 157
Greenhill, Basil, 98
Gropius, Walter, 136
Grundy, Reverend C.H., 166
Guided Walks, 37
Hall, Tim, 132
Hamilton, Lady Emma, 86, 88
Harrison, Frederick, 164
Hasker, A.A., 140
Healey, Denis, 166
Heaton, Ronald, 164
Helter Skelter bookshop, 175, 185
Hendrix, Jimi, 14
Henrey, Mrs. Robert, 154
Herber, Mark, 45
Heritage
  ideas of, 15
  awards, 51
  competitions, 52
  display of, 52
  genealogical, 108
  industry, 66, 69, 76–77, 86, 129
  landscape, 65–79
  proud, 134
  pub, 156
  site, 15, 65, 76, 83
  souvenirs, 86
  stamps, 52
Hess, Myra, 166
Hewison, Robert, 86, 87
History from below, 14, 139
History Workshop, 16
  Journal 167
Hitchcock, Alfred, 32
Hobsbawm, Eric, 44, 49
Hoggart, Richard, 135, 136
Holbein's 'Ambassadors' 30
Holland, Patricia, 21, 24, 26
Holyoake, George Jacob, 151, 161
Hornsby, Laurie, 134
Howell, George, 151, 161, 163
Huxley, Thomas, 39
Identity(ies)
  aspects of, 129
  assertions of, 129
  constructions of, 15, 105, 106
  cultural, 105, 107, 137, 176
  family, 17
  minority, 152
  local, 127, 138
  national, 129, 130
  and urban spaces, 127–148
Inquest Committees, 157
Institute of Heraldic and Genealogical Studies, 45
Institute of Historical Research, 13
International Women and the Sea Network, 88, 96
International Workingmen's Association

(1866–69), 161
Internet, 13
  and music, 175, 182, 183
Jaques, Henry, 112
Jessop, Violet, 90
Jewson, Esther Lydia Furley, aka 'Lydia', 37–50
Jewson, Gerald Arthur, 37, 42, 46
Jewson, William Arthur, 37–50
John, Angela V., 39
Johnny and Jack, 180
Jones, Sian, 83, 91, 95
Jordan, Louis, 172
Kammen, Carol, 146
Karp, Ivan 144
Kavanagh, Gaynor, 92, 93, 95, 98, 99
Keiller, Alexander, 67, 68, 69, 76
  museum, 73, 74
Kelly, Sir Gerald, 27
Kelmscott Press, The, 161
Kennet District Council, 75
King, Ken, 75
Knowles, Sir Francis and Lady, 75
Lacan, Jacques, 91, 95
Lackham College, 74
Lamarr, Mark, 176
Lantz, Brian, 145
Laughton, Charles, 32
League Against Cruel Sports, 56
Lees-Milne, James, 69
Lens(es) conceptual use in discussion, 38, 43, 98, 100
Leppert, Richard, 31
Liberty and Property League, 157
Library Association of the United Kingdom, 163
Limouzin, Nellie, 42, 43
Liner notes, 179, 182
Livingstone, Dandy, 178
London Chamber of Commerce, 157
London Co-operative Society, 151
London County Council Choral Union, 41, 46
London and Middlesex Archaeological Society, 163
London Orchestral Society, 41
Lovell, Elsie, 46
Luv'd Ones, The (rock band), 177
'Lydia', see Jewson, Esther Lydia Furley
McCartney, Paul, 14
MacDonald, Ramsay, 161
Manzoni, Herbert, 136
Maps, 107, 111, 114, 115, 120, 134, 162
Maritime
  historians, 96
  history, 86, 96
  historiography, 16, 85–98
  womens history, 96, 82
  museology, 87
  museums, 81–103
Marley, Bob, 178
Marvel Records, 171
Massingham, Harold John, 56
Mason, Raymond, 130
Mayhew, Henry, 135
Mechanics Institute, 158
Memory(ies), 72, 95, 96, 110
  remembering as a constructive activity, 95
  and forgetting, 22, 33, 95, 136,140
Merseybeat, 175
Merseyside Maritime Museum, 89, 90
  and Lifelines Gallery, 90
Middleton, A.D., 54, 57

Ministry of Agriculture, 57, 58
  and Fisheries, 59
Ministry of Works, 71
Mistry, Dhruva, 130
Mitchell, W.J.T., 22
Mojo, 16, 175
Moore, Henry, 68
Morgan, Dai, 30
Morgan, Mary Jane, 25, 28, 30
Morgan, Trevor, 19, 20, 23, 33
Morris, William, 159
Museum(s), 13, 14, 39, 83, 144, 158–159
  For specific museums see under alphabetical heading
  North Woolwich station reborn as, 119
  practice, 88
  shops, 88.
Museum of the Jewellery Quarter (Birmingham), 131
Museum of Wiltshire Rural Life, 74
National Anti-Grey Squirrel Campaign, 58, 59
National Fishing Heritage Centre, Grimsby, 94
National Maritime Museum, 88, 89, 99
  and Customs and Excise Gallery, 90
National Portrait Gallery, 31
National Secular Society, 151
National Trust, 14, 58, 65–79
  Reserve in Formby, 60
Navy League, 157, 161
Nelson, Admiral, 84, 86, 88
  Lady, 86
Newcastle Weekly Chronicle, 163
New England Teen Scene, 182
Newham Recorder, 120
Nineteenth Amendment, The (pop group, see The Exotics)
NPI (National Provident Institution), 51
Open University, 48
Orr, Linda, 33
Orwell, George, 42, 129, 135
Other, The, 61, 100
Otherness, 40, 100, 142, 146
Owens, Janet, 99
Oxenham, Patrick, 52
Pagenstecher, Dr., 107, 117
Pama Records, 178
Pankhurst, Emmeline, 43
Pattern 23 Theatre Company, 131
Pay, Sharon, 83, 91, 95
Pearce, Susan, 91
Pevsner, Nikolaus, 65
Photographs, 15, 18–35, 69, 72, 73, 93, 140
Pincombe, W.J., 165
Polydor Chronicles, 175
Porter, Gaby, 86, 90, 91, 94, 95, 100
Porter, Roy, 112
Portishead (pop group), 173
Postcards
  of Scottish wildlife, 60, 61
  of Avebury, 73
  of Emma Hamilton, 89
  of a migrating mother, 89
  Traders, 44
Powell, Enoch, 142
Presence
  black people's, 178
  Women (and the sea), 83
  City of London workers, 156
Presley, Elvis, 172
Priestly, J.B., 135
Proctor, Wayne, 184

Puffin Club, The, 162
Queen Mother, Queen Elizabeth the, Elizabeth Bowes-Lyon, 27, 31
Queenspark Books, 139
Quercus Books, 141
Quinn, May, 81 99
Rabbit Clearance Societies, 59
Radio, 13, 183
Radley, Alan, 96
Rainwater, Marvin, 180
Ramblers Association, 56
Randall, E.D., 56
Rational recreation movement, 114
Read, Mary, 98
Record collecting, 171
Record Collector, 16, 175
Redskins, The (rock group), 178
Reggae, 173, 178–179
Resistance
  to change, 129, 132, 136
  to geographical symmetry, 153
  to technology, 172, 175
Roberts, John, 141
Robins, Kevin, 129, 132
Rogers, William, 156, 157, 164
Rolling Stones, 172, 184
Rosbotham, Samue,l 58
Rosebery, Lord, 157, 158, 161
Rowbotham, Sheila, 13
Rowntree, Seebohm, 140
Royal Naval Museum, 86, 88
Royal Society for the Prevention of Accidents (RoSPA), 53–54
Royal Society for the Protection of Birds (RSPB), 58
Royal Zoological Society of Scotland, 60
Ruskin College Public History Group, 14, 35n21, 185n3
Sadlers Wells Ballet, 130
Samuel, Raphael, 14,16, 20, 60, 151, 162, 167, 168
  archive, 168
  Centre For Metropolitan History, 16, 168
See For Miles Records, 171
Self
  consciousness, 24, 40
  the additional, 40
  the historical, 13
  conceptions of a located, 41
  construction of, 24, 133–134
  esteem, 44
  improvement, 157
  notion of, 48
  perception, 152
  presentation, 152, 162
  studies, 49
  a wider, 121
  the popular, 120, 121
Shakleton, Ernest, 165
Shakespeare, William, 139
She (rock band,) 177
Sims, George, 166
Skinheads 178–179
Skinheads Against Racial Prejudice (SHARP), 178
Slave trade, 178
Smith, Reverend A.C., 68
Smith, Charles Roach, 158
Smith, W.H., 13
Snell, Hannah, 98
Snow, Edward Rowe, 98
Socialist Standard, The, 161

Society of Antiquaries, 163
Society of Genealogists, 44
Society for Public Libraries, 163
Sony Corporation, 172
South Wales Borderers, 23, 30
Spectator, The, 166
Spence, Jo, 26
Stafford, Carole Ann, 141
Stark, Suzanne, J., 98
Steedman, Carolyn, 26, 39, 49
Steel, David, 166
Stewardess(ing), 81, 87, 89, 90, 99
Stukeley, William, 67, 68, 71, 72
Swainson, L., 59
Swing Riots (1830), 68
Talbot, Ann, 98
Tar(s), Jill and Jack, 86, 88, 99
Television, 13, 14, 183
Thomas, Gilbert, 166
Thorne, James, 116
Thorne, Will, 119
Timewriting, 39
Tillett, Ben, 119
Tindal Street Memory Group, 139
Tissot, James, 87
Topography (ies), 37, 38, 105, 111
  Toponymy, 106, 111, 118, 119, 120
  Toponyms, 107 110, 114, 115, 121
Townsend, Charles Harrison, 152
Toynbee Hall, 154
Trades Union Congress, 154
The Tremelons (pop group, *see* Lu'v'd Ones)
Trojan Records, 178
Tufty Club, The, 52, 53
Tull, Malcolm, 97
Unconscious (the), 40
Unselfconscious(ness), 38
  and history writing, 39, 133, 146
Urry, John, 99
Value (notions of), 91
Vincent, David, 140
Vinnedge, Char(lotte), 177
Vinyl as a recording medium 171–189
Volkoff, Janis, 177
Voltaire, 39
Wallas, Graham, 161
Wardmotes, 157
Warner Archives, 175
Warren, Tony, 136
Webb, David, 163
Weize, Richard, 179–180
Western, Johnny, 180
West Ham United Football Club, 119, 121
Westside Records, 174
We The People (rock band, *see* Proctor, Wayne)
White, Hayden, 33
Whitechapel Library, 154
White Hart Public House, 156
Wildwood Records, 177
Williams, David, 87
Williams, Gwen, 131
Williams, Gwyn .A., 28
Williams, Mary-Louise, 84, 90, 98
Williams, Raymond, 135
Williamson, Henry, 56
Wiltshire Rural Life Society, 74
Woking Musical Society, 41
Women in Heritage Archives and Museums! (WHAM!), 97
Workers Education Association, 158
Wright, Patrick, 52